The Goddess Orgasm

Also by Eve Marx

What's Your Sexual IQ?

The
Goddess Orgasm

Empowered Sex for Today's Woman

Eve Marx

CITADEL PRESS
Kensington Publishing Corp.
www.kensingtonbooks.com

CITADEL PRESS BOOKS are published by

Kensington Publishing Corp.
850 Third Avenue
New York, NY 10022

All Kensington titles, imprints, and distributed lines are available at special quantity discounts for bulk purchases for sales promotions, premiums, fund-raising, educational, or institutional use. Special book excerpts or customized printings can also be created to fit specific needs. For details, write or phone the office of the Kensington special sales manager: Kensington Publishing Corp., 850 Third Avenue, New York, NY 10022, attn: Special Sales Department; phone 1-800-221-2647.

CITADEL PRESS and the Citadel logo are Reg. U.S. Pat. & TM Off.

First printing: February 2005

10 9 8 7 6 5 4 3 2 1

Printed in the United States of America

Library of Congress Control Number: 2004113761

ISBN 0-8065-2666-1

This book would be nothing without the great Greeks—
in particular, mighty Aphrodite, the Goddess of Love, and
Artemis, virgin Goddess of the Hunt.

Contents

Acknowledgments

Thank you, thank you, a thousand times thank you to my fantastic and generous editor, Bob Shuman, who enlivens me, encourages me, directs me, and guides me. Bob, you are the best. I also want to thank my incredibly goddessy agent, June Clark, for her uproarious sense of humor, her fine insights, and her incredible anecdotes that helped keep me writing long into the night. I hugely appreciate the generosity and patience of my goddess girlfriends, especially the ones who agreed to fill out the questionnaire, and for sharing so freely. Most of all, I thank my amusing muse, the horseman, C., whose candid conversations, charming barn, amazing horses, and aromatic tack room inspired me and kept the vibe going.

Introduction

According to the stories of the *Iliad*, Aphrodite, who sprung from the sea, was a "modest and lovely goddess" whose gentle domain was intended to be the sweetness of love. But sweet Aphrodite was also randy and promiscuous, and at times got into trouble that was deep. Although the great god Zeus advised her to "concern herself only with the lovely secrets of marriage," Aphrodite had other ideas.

In the *Odyssey* of Homer, a singer tells the tale of how Aphrodite and her illicit lover Aries secretly laid together in the bed of Aphrodite's husband, Lord Hephaestus. Helios, the sun, spied on the lovers and tattled to Hephaestus, who asked a blacksmith to devise a clever fastening that would ensnare and hold the lovers in an unbreakable trap. So involved were they in their lovemaking that the careless couple fell into the trap. Hephaestus stood enraged with the other Olympians as witnesses and demanded his gifts of courtship be returned. It was only after Poseidon offered to pay damages that Hephaestus agreed to loose the bonds. After she was set free, Aphrodite traveled to her sacred precinct on the island of Cyprus where she was bathed by the Graces, while her lover Aries traveled on to Thrace. Having seen the two lovers in the indignity of the snare, the god Apollo asked another god, Hermes, how he would feel in such a situation. Hermes responded that he would gladly suffer three times the number of bonds if only he could share the bed of Aphrodite. Such was the sexual aura and thrall of the mighty Aphrodite, with whom every man, both mortal and god, wished to share an orgasm.

What really is an orgasm? One dictionary defines it as the moment of most intense pleasure experienced during sexual intercourse. Another describes it as the highest point of sexual excitement, characterized by strong feelings of pleasure and marked normally by the ejaculation of semen. I don't know about you, but I find both these descriptions limiting. Why restrict one of the most incredible pleasures a person can experience to an act linked with something you can only do with another person (i.e., sexual intercourse), or a physiological sensation addressing males only (women, obviously, don't ejaculate semen)? Even the word "moment" in the first definition bothers me, because in my studying of orgasm and from my own orgasmic experiences, I know that magic moment of intense pleasure can last so much longer.

When I started writing this book, I realized I was tackling territory that has been gone into many times before. The Hindu yogis figured out that masturbating but delaying orgasm resulted in a more intense orgasm when they finally let one arrive. The sex researchers Masters and Johnson studied orgasm ad nauseam to write their book *Human Sexual Response*, published in 1966. We even know that while a human orgasm lasts only a few moments, pigs can have orgasms lasting up to half an hour. Orgasm, or the Big O, as many women's magazines (and more than a few male-oriented titles) call it, is a hot topic. We're lucky to be living in a time when our culture is so fascinated by the concept of personal satisfaction. We are living in a time when many, many people are focused on what it means to "Get Mine!"

I realized that while the media and popular culture have created an atmosphere and perception that every person is experiencing mind-blowing, extraordinary sexual experiences and fantastic orgasms on a regular, even daily, basis, the reality is that many women feel they are missing out. They feel their orgasms, if they are having them, are ho-hum, mundane. They might be "good enough," but in a world driven by the concepts of "bigger is better," and "supersize that," they feel, quite rightly, that they shouldn't have to settle for a "good enough" orgasm.

And they don't have to!

The Goddess Orgasm is all about giving you a bigger, better, longer lasting, more meaningful orgasm. In other words, a goddess orgasm—an experience of intense sexual pleasure fit for . . . a goddess.

There are a lot of statistics available on the topic of female orgasms. Doctors and scientists doing research at recognized institutes of sexual study—The ABS (American Board of Sexology), the NIH (National Institutes of Health) and the Kinsey Institute for Research in Sex, Gender and Reproduction, to name a few—spend their workdays calculating nipple size and counting orgasms. It's in vogue these days to break even quasi-mystical personally transformational experiences such as orgasm down to the driest mathematical and scientific explanation, as though we're all just numbers. If you are a number freak, or someone who gets a big rush from accumulating data, information like how many calories a thirty-minute session of intercourse will burn (150 calories, for the record), how long the female orgasm lasts (on the average, a few seconds), or how many times a woman can climax during a single lovemaking session (infinite), this is not necessarily the book for you. My approach, based on my years of writing about sex for magazines including *Penthouse*, *Swank*, and many women's service magazines, interviewing porn actors and actresses, studying sexual techniques, absorbing the so-called bible of sex, the *Kama Sutra*, and authoring myriad sexual "how-to" articles and two sex advice books, as well as interviewing (both officially and unofficially) regular, everyday living women about their sex lives, I know that a woman's orgasm cannot be based or described solely on physiological or reflexive physical response. I'm really insulted when anyone describes an orgasm as a "crotch sneeze"! The female sexual climax, like the larger arena of sex itself, is mysterious. And it's not the same for every woman, or even every goddess.

What deeply interests me about orgasms is how women have them, the different kinds of orgasms a woman can have, their self-pleasuring routines, their sexual fantasies, if they've found their G-spot. To find these things out, I enlisted the help of many women I know and some I don't know at all. I created a questionnaire that I personally handed out or managed to get into the hands of many women and felt blessed that such numbers of them were so forthcoming in their responses. The questions I asked were very, very personal, so personal that I shielded the identities of the respondents even from myself by changing their names and any identifying characteristics.

I loved the idea that smart, sexually savvy women—modern goddesses—could share the details of what works sexually for them, even very technical information, with other women. Reading the responses, I saw that every woman does not achieve orgasm the same way. *The Goddess Orgasm* is about sharing information, introducing women readers to what works for and fulfills another woman and to new ways that they can feel fulfilled.

C., a male friend, my muse, actually (and yes, I do have a muse—doesn't every goddess?), once remarked to me that the women I surround myself with all possess some quality of goddessness. And that is why I enlisted their help in the creation of this book.

Much of the information shared in *The Goddess Orgasm* is explicit. Some of it is frankly erotic. There is a reason for this. I think the more comfortable I can make another woman feel about her own sexuality, the more likely it is that she will be able to enjoy her orgasms. While there certainly are women who are stymied from achieving the full pleasure they deserve because of physiological or even emotional issues, I believe that, for the most part, women do have control over their own bodies to the extent that they can orchestrate their own orgasms. Having a partner or being in love with someone who is dedicated to bringing you to orgasm is nice, but it isn't a necessity. As women, we have the resources at hand and within ourselves to create our own orgasms, and to define and refine our own pleasure.

Helen Fisher, an anthropologist affiliated with Rutgers University and author of *Anatomy of Love* (1992) and *Why We Love: The Nature and Chemistry of Romantic Love* (2004), has written on the topic of functional magnetic resonance images (FMRIs) of the brains of subjects who were deeply in love. Medical technology has now advanced to a place where photographic images of the brain can show us how our brains work in regard to love and lust. The scientific and medical evidence points to three distinct brain circuits that govern our love lives, each with its own chemical imprint. Lust is ruled in both men and women by the sex hormone testosterone. Romantic love is governed by the neurotransmitter, or brain chemical, dopamine. What Fisher calls "attachment," the calm bond between longtime mates, is stimulated by the brain chemicals oxytocin in females and vasopressin in men.

As we are humans and not machines, our circuits do get crossed. This is why we can feel deeply connected to a longtime partner, have a crush on the kid who bags our groceries, and simultaneously enjoy a wild sex fantasy that springs full-blown from what we can imagine in our heads, all at the same time. In fact, our ultimate—that is to say, our goddess—orgasms can arise from this crossed-circuit state.

James Hollis is a therapist and author of a "Jungian perspective on relationships," *The Middle Passage: From Misery to Meaning in Midlife*, and *Tracking the Gods: The Place of Myth in Modern Life*. In his scholarly paper "The Eden Project: In Search of the Magical Other," he states: "What the gods ask most of us is that we attend to them, bear conscious witness to their energies of which their forms are but the material husk. If we do not serve that depth of energy which a god represents in whatever erotic act, then we have violated something profound." We are more than simply bodies or material husks. Our ability to have orgasms is a gift possibly given to us by God and the gods. The body is the temple of the soul. Orgasm is about renewal, rejuvenation, release. We can experience joy, pleasure, even communion with another person through our climactic experiences. Let's make the most of this gift, and in doing so, become more goddess-like.

Prologue

I'd like to share this true tale. A while back, I was invited to a party. It was a party for women, no men allowed. Even the large and elegant canine companion of the beautiful and sexy hostess was a bitch! This party is an annual event that has been going on for several years. It is an open secret that sooner or later some (if not most!) of the conversation at this party will turn to sex. One year, all the women sat in a circle on the floor and regaled each other with the stories of how they came to give up their virginity. I already knew I was going to be writing this book, and I mentioned to the hostess that I thought talking about it would be a wonderful way for the women at the party to ask questions and share their knowledge about orgasm—in other words, engage in a wide-open information exchange. It's worth mentioning, however, that the hostess phoned me the morning of the party to warn me that some of the guests might be uncomfortable discussing the topic. I mentioned the phone call to another woman, my friend Chloe, who immediately responded, and I quote, "The reason so many women don't know anything about orgasm is that they're afraid to talk about it—even among themselves. And what a pity that is!"

She's right. That is a pity. Many people staunchly believe that all the intimate information about sex and orgasm a female should receive about this essential portion of her human nature is from her mother. It's great for you if it happens that way. A great deal of the information I got about sex I did learn from my mother, a sex goddess if there ever was one. Mostly I learned from her through observation. My mother, Geraldine, had many suitors. She was married four times. Only once was she divorced; her other husbands, including her first husband who was one of her true loves, my father, she lost to heart attack or cancer. Although Geraldine enjoyed her friendship with several close and simpatico women friends, other rare ladies who possessed their own goddess auras, it was men, en masse, who were drawn to her, and I don't just mean sexually. Some message she was sending, consciously or not I will never really know, was like a whistle that only men heard. I am certain she was aware of it; she could adjust it, vary its intensity. Sometimes she turned it down very low, while at other times she pushed it way up so that it was like a siren call. When Geraldine put it out there, men came running.

They wanted to help her. They offered her their hands. They did her bidding and her favors. It wasn't necessary for her to be lovers with these men for them to love her. I remember seeing men bending over to kiss her hand. Walking beside her down the main avenue of the town I grew up in, I sometimes noticed men's otherwise stony faces relaxing as they strode by, taking her in. Was it her walk, I wondered, that attracted them so? No one could ever see her eyes, shielded in all weathers in dark glasses. In public, she was a mystery. Her truly private life I can only conjecture about, since it all happened behind closed doors.

I am sorry to say that some of the other lessons I took in from this awesome goddess, who just happened to be my mother, are ones I've spent a lifetime unlearning. Some of them were really hurtful. Following the cultural rules and customs of Jewish females, the tribal community she herself was raised in, my mother celebrated the news that I had become a woman and had begun my periods by slapping me as hard as she could across my face.

That wasn't the beginning of my shame. As a very young child, I innocently touched myself between my legs after my bathtub discovery that such touching felt good. My mother shouted to me never to do that. Years later, when she walked in on me by accident in my bedroom as I was pleasuring myself, she went ballistic and beat me. And yet my mother sent me endless sexual messages about how I was to convey and purport myself, buying me fashionable, provocative clothing that showed off my adolescent curves. She encouraged the use of makeup. Even as she helped to develop certain aspects of my nascent sex-goddessness, she was simultaneously driven to shame me and crush other evidences of my sexuality. To this day, I believe she did this because she understood how powerful female sexuality is and worried what I might do with it.

Many openly sexy, extraordinary women volunteered to share their thoughts about orgasm with me in order to write this book. They were willing to allow me to pool their knowledge, their sex secrets, their tips, their favorite techniques to rouse and bring forth the penultimate female sexual experience—orgasm. I have been very lucky how forthcoming, straightshooting, and honest my goddesses have been.

Let me tell you something about these women. First of all, to insure their privacy and confidentiality, all of their names have been changed. All of the women are employed in a professional capacity. Any identifying characteristics, other than their marital status, have been altered to guarantee their anonymity. Their responses to my very personal and probing questions, however, have not been changed. Their words are their own. As you will see, they were very candid.

Erica is in her early thirties. She is married, has two children, and works in the field of mental health. Roxanne, a school librarian, is in her early forties. She has three children and is divorced. She is actively dating and has had several marriage proposals, all of which she has, so far, turned down. Carole is an executive secretary in her mid-forties and is married with two nearly grown children. Elizabeth is a fundraiser for a large nonprofit organization. She is in her early fifties and, at the time of this writing, in the process of getting divorced. Chelsea, in her late twenties, is an artist and a single city gal. Taryn is also in her late twenties. She is a schoolteacher, recently married, and expecting her first child. Helaine is in her mid-forties, was in sales, took a fantastic buy-out offer from her company, and is enjoying her married life. She has one nearly grown child. Serena is nearly sixty, divorced, an artist. Samantha is an editor in her early forties, divorced, and has one child. Suzette owns her own public relations agency, is in her mid-sixties, divorced, and has a rather famous grown child. Betsy is an events planner in her mid-forties, married, and has two adolescent children. Shane is a journalist in her early thirties, divorced, and has no children. Vanessa is forty years old, married, has two teenaged daughters, and is a graphic designer. Lucia is a lawyer. She is in her mid-forties and has two children, a boy and a girl. Jolie is in her mid-twenties, a professional dancer, and very happily single. Jamie is in her late twenties, divorced, and works as a veterinary assistant. Chloe is fifty years old, divorced, and has a prominent position in the art world. Juilianna is in her mid-fifties, is bisexual and divorced. Joyce, Riva, Ann, Jill, Claudia, Bela, Sela, Kendra, Jane, Leslie, Christine, Carmen and Ava are all women I met briefly and whom I told about this book who agreed to answer a few questions and share their thoughts and wisdom on the topic.

A handful of men participated in my study, all of them, save one, friends of mine. I have also taken the liberty of changing their names to protect their privacy. In the book they are referred to as Peter, Keith, Curt, Twan, Glenn, Mack, Alec, Jake and Mel. Mel is actually Samantha's lover, although she said she never saw his responses to the questionnaire.

The Goddess Orgasm is a book about the ultimate sex act. There are many wonderful, even transformational sex acts that can turn your head, spin you around, leave you gasping. But you might not have an orgasm from any of them, or not every time you test-drive one. What is important is for you as a woman to recognize what is special about orgasm, to honor and revere it for the beautiful and unique gift that it is.

PART I

Preparing for Goddessex

Always wear one garment that is sexy. You don't always have to show cleavage. The sexy garment could be your black fishnet trouser socks.

—Goddess motto

What Kind of Goddess Are You?

*T*he Greeks embraced immortal goddesses and mythologized them so devotedly that even today women honor and are inspired by them. The Greek goddesses were radiant. They looked very much like mortal women and, in some ways, behaved like them, being prone to fits of jealousy. For example, Hera, wife of Zeus, terrified him with her jealous rages. Athena was wrathful; miffed by the talent of another goddess—Arachne—at the loom, Athena struck her on the head and turned her into a spider. Sometimes they got a bit hung up on their finery (think of Aphrodite's attachment to her gold girdle). At the same time, the goddesses were great heroines.

The Greeks believed that goddesses lived alongside male gods on top of Olympus, a mountain so high no mortal being could climb it. Occasionally, the gods and goddesses descended the mountain to visit Earth, where they secretively mingled with the mortals. Athena, the goddess of wisdom, was known for her skills in warfare. She arrived on Mount Olympus, sprung full-grown from the head of her father, Zeus. Delicate Aurora was the goddess of the dawn. Artemis, also known as Diana—my personal favorite—was the virgin goddess of the moon and the hunt. Artemis/Diana asked her father, the great Zeus, to promise that she would never have to wed. She remained forever in the woods living the life of a wild child.

The Romans worshipped Venus, the goddess of love. When the Greeks defeated the Romans, Venus became known as Aphrodite.

In the Greek legend, stunning Aphrodite had no mother or father. She arrived on the plume of the West Wind, rising out of the sea on a cushion of foam. The three Graces, nymph goddesses of great beauty, became Aphrodite's handmaidens, dressed her in shimmering garments, and carried her to Olympus in a golden chariot drawn by white doves.

When the gods and goddesses first laid eyes on Aphrodite, they were instantly smitten, quickly making her one of their own. Zeus was so nervous about the prospect of all the male gods fighting over her that he quickly selected Hephaestus to be her husband, who in turn gifted her with a lavish gold girdle. The garment turned out to be a mistake; when Aphrodite wore it, no man could resist her, and she was already deliciously irresistible.

Other cultures have their own goddesses. The Hindus worshipped a goddess of sex and love, Shakti. The Buddhists revere a love goddess known as Yami. The Phoenicians had Ashtarte. The Egyptians admired Hathor. The Central American peoples, the Aztecs and the Mayans, worshipped Erzuli, Lady of Love, and Loa, the Beautiful Lady, and made sacrifices to a powerful feminine goddess they called Oloso, or the Lady Crocodile. She was a hot one, but she could eat a man alive!

There are plenty of modern (and mortal) goddesses worthy of contemplation. Certainly Natalie Wood was a goddess, as was Marilyn Monroe. Hollywood has always searched out and actively cultivated divine figures: Lana Turner, Rita Hayworth, and Greta Garbo instantly spring to mind. Charlotte Rampling even in her late fifties is still a goddess. If you doubt this, check her out in the movie *Swimming Pool*.

The erotic writer Colette was clearly a goddess. Before she married Ted Turner, Jane Fonda was a goddess, or at least the character she played in the film *Klute*, was one. Some goddesses are completely fictional. Think of the character Maggie played by Elizabeth Taylor in *Cat on a Hot Tin Roof*, or the nymphet goddess Lo in *Lolita*, both brought to life through the power of imagination springing from a writer's head.

We all know some mortal goddess who left a mark on our lives. Channel yourself back to mighty women from your past. For me, that would start with Marguerite and Teeny, two very different but incredibly powerful black women who were charged with raising me. Or the mother of my best friend, who encouraged us girls to try on her furs and evening gowns. When I think of the beautiful and fascinating women who intrigued me, and analyze exactly what it was about them that made them so compelling, it always comes back to their combination of strength and goodness, plus an aura of eroticism they possessed that perfumed the very air they walked in.

I love recalling other sexy goddesses who even briefly entered my life, such as my Uncle Charlie's third wife, Barbara, whose exploits and reputation were legends. Or my first city friend, a woman named Eve, who was also the first person I'd ever met with whom I shared a name. Eve was like a sister to me, though a somewhat raunchier, more liberated sister. A painter of gouaches, one day she quit shaving her armpits; you'd be surprised how many men found her underarm hair an aphrodisiac! I had a sculptor friend, S., a tall, redheaded goddess who abandoned consorting with men, but who didn't choose women either. She was the first woman who told me about vibrators.

My friend Meg taught me how to be more at ease with myself and also how to dress and decorate for Goddessex. Her bedroom floor was completely covered with silk lingerie and her piles of kicked-off cowboy boots. I love the energy of the women who work the counter at my favorite hometown coffee bar. I think about the beautiful young women I've seen still in their heavenly nymph stage, radiating healthful sexual energy as they waft past me on the street. Goddesses are everywhere, if only you look for them. Now let the orgasms begin!

Virgin Orgasms: The First Awakening of the Goddess

*B*efore you are a goddess, first you are a nymph. As a very young girl, the boundaries between what is sexual and what is sensual are quite fluid. They ebb and flow around each other, and it is difficult to say which is which. Young goddesses—nymphs—don't necessarily interpret their earliest erotic experiences as sex. You shouldn't leap to fasten a label on your early erotic experiences. To do so is distinctly an American issue. In France, where girls of thirteen are openly reckoned to be nymphs, this baby-step phase of goddess womanhood is celebrated as an awakening, a subtle but growing recognition of bodily pleasures.

Channel yourself back to when you were a young girl. Return to your earliest experiences and remembrances of when you first began touching yourself. Put yourself back in the time when you first recognized the power of your own hand and the sensation of bedclothes or something else you rubbed against that gave you pleasure. Many young goddesses recall lying in their beds on warm summer nights, discovering for the first time the delicious feel of cool, smooth sheets on bare, heated flesh. Or they discovered by accident the sweetly pleasurable erotic feelings they got "down there" from leaning against something warm and vibrating, like the family's washing machine. Whether by accident or design, at some point every young woman is awakened to her own budding sexuality and learns that she holds the power to give herself an orgasm. This discovery leads her further into the world of self-pleasuring.

The virgin orgasm is very intense because it is steeped in a cloud of mystery. Most of us can barely remember the first time we touched ourselves. We only know that once we started, we didn't want to stop. A young girl's discovery of her ability to pleasure herself is truly a turning point in any nymph goddess's life. The virgin orgasm, intensely personal and mostly unshared as an experience, sadly is regarded as unsavory, shameful, something that must be denied. Even very sexually experienced adult women are reluctant to share their most intimate stories of how they discovered their orgasms and how they pleasured themselves. Even in all-female gatherings, discussion of the topic of virgin orgasms is nearly always taboo. I am going to break that taboo now.

We live in a time when the idealized sexual experience always involves another person. The fact is that most women discover their orgasm on their own, and usually by their own hand. Here's what Shane had to say about her earliest orgasm experiences.

Shane: *As a young sex goddess growing up, from an early age I was experiencing little thrills, trills of pleasure that clearly were connected to the realm of erotica. I was transfixed by certain actors on certain television shows, feelings I now understand to be nascent harbingers of sexual fetishes and stimuli that have excited me for a lifetime. It's a little embarrassing to admit, but I was definitely aroused by the cowboy characters who appeared on the myriad TV westerns of the 1960s. I didn't have the language or the vocabulary yet to explain my feelings or the sensations my body experienced as my eyes remained riveted to the screen. These brawny bastions of American manhood who wore rough jeans and leather chaps, who boldly rode horses and lassoed and took down bawling steers, stirred my imagination and sent chills down my still-childish spine. Luckily, I never developed any fetish for some of their other Wild West accoutrements—such as spitting tobacco and shooting guns—but I have no doubt that some other young girls watching those programs found some of those hardboiled cowboy elements invigorating, if not downright intoxicating.*

Intoxicating is a good way to describe those sensations I felt while eyeballing Doug McClure, the actor who played the character Trampas on *The Virginian*. All Doug had to do was smile his lazy smile as he hung around the bunkhouse, one hip sexily cocked. On the most elemental level, the sensations I experienced were purely physiological. My mouth went a little dry. My tummy tightened up. I felt a vague stirring in what romance writers would rightly call "my loins." Today, I couldn't relate a single plotline or incident from that show, although I can summon up a complete recollection of Doug McClure's smile and exactly how I related to it. His smile reached out through our black-and-white television set into my family's living room and grabbed me where I lay on the couch watching him. His smile was like an arrow or a speeding bullet straight to my groin. I felt something akin to a physical pain from the shock of it. I still recall squirming and rubbing my thighs together watching him in a hypnotized, nearly narcotic state. On the evenings that *The Virginian* aired, I spent the hour in a trance, grateful to be told it was time to go to bed, relief finally found alone in my narrow bed, when I was free to devote twenty or so minutes to daydreaming about my love idol. While I was still years away from actual masturbation and orgasm, the tingling sensations I recognized in my body in response to this man were definitely erotic in nature.

Helaine, Carole and Jolie described similar experiences.

Helaine: *I touched myself and, yes, I did fantasize and had full-blown movies in my head about what I thought sexual foreplay might be. I think I brought myself to orgasm for the first time when I was about thirteen. I thought the touching/tingling when first discovered was amazing, and I couldn't believe people didn't talk about it like they did the weather.*

Carole: *What I noticed from the time that I was about seven was that touching the area between my legs made me feel funny, made me yearn* *somehow, but I wasn't sure for what. I remember walking around wearing my mom's Kotex pressed between my legs, no fantasies, just that the pressure felt good. At age eleven, when I first perched over the bidet in Austria, I was just curious, and I had an orgasm so fast I didn't have a chance to think about anything other than "Ooooooooooooh this feels good!" before my knees buckled and I nearly fell over post-orgasm. I don't think I had any fantasies, because I am visual and have a photographic memory and had never seen people making love or anything other than Playboy centerfolds (my dad's). So masturbating, I just liked how it felt, and the sensations were enough to get me off. I imagine it was after my first kiss, when I was thirteen (he was an eighteen-year-old Spaniard from Barcelona), that I began using someone/something (kissing/petting) to fantasize about.*

Jolie: *The first time I remember having orgasm was by touching myself as a little girl. I was about four or five years old. I was lying flat on my stomach on the floor, playing with puzzles or dolls or whatever. I noticed that pressing my pelvis against the floor with some pressure created a very pleasurable sensation. And if I scissored my legs at this time, I would experience a "burst" of pleasure—basically, an orgasm. Needless to say, this was a very cool discovery, which I exercised on occasion. Sometimes I would put my hands inside my "Days of the Week" panties and finger myself a little, too. At such a young, tender age, I didn't have any fantasies associated with doing this—it was more about the sensation and process. I do remember playing at my best friend's house when I was around six years old. We were on the floor playing a board game when I asked her if it "felt good" for her to rub herself against the floor (we were actually on her carpet). She said it did, and I recall us masturbating together several times. We even had contests to see who could come first!*

Fantasy, even at an early age, for many young girls and virginal women plays an essential role in the creation of erotic and orgasmic sensations. Here Jamie shares her earliest sexual fantasy in rich detail.

Jamie: *One of my own earliest and long-enduring fantasies that I entertained myself with several times a week involved me in the role of a Native American beauty, probably Pocahantas. Initially, my fantasy was limited mostly to an imagined costume I wore, a soft buckskin dress decorated with beads and fringe, knee-high soft leather moccasins, and a elaborately beaded belt. In my fantasy, my hair was very long (in reality, my mother forced me to endure what was called a "pixie cut") and loose and fell sexily about my face, although I was too young at the time to even know the word "sexy." Amazingly, I never envisioned any kind of undergarment worn beneath this dress. The earliest versions of the fantasy involved a male . . . sometimes a young Native American boy with smooth supple skin, at other times a White Man soldier or an outlaw or some kind of desperado . . . lifting my skirt. Initially, the single exposure of my knees alone was enough to send my fingers racing to the panties that I always wore beneath my nightgown. For a long time, I never dared touch my actual flesh, but only caressed myself through the veil of my cotton panties, thick, heavy, absorbent ones, which helpfully served to soak up the moisture already flowing from me. My first efforts at self-pleasure were tentative and austere. I would cup the entire palm of my hand over my vulva, just enough to permit the heat and slight pressure of my hand to further warm my pudenda, sometimes squeezing my fingers around the whole area to gently press together the lips. My earliest masturbatory impulses had more to do with squeezing the engorged flesh together, rather than to try to open it up. This slight squeezing and pressure sent minor convulsions coursing through my body, electrifying it without burning it up. I believe I was experiencing tiny ripples of orgasm, because after five, ten, or fifteen minutes of this kind of stimulation, my heart would begin pumping harder and my breath would become shallow and my legs would stiffen and my back would arch. Goose pimples frequently broke out over my entire body at the most* *extreme moment. At the peak of my pleasure—a climax that lasted for several dramatic, intoxicating seconds—I would experience a surge of powerful energy vibrating through me, an electric current that was almost like a shock. The very instant it was over, my entire body would relax and go limp, and I would be able to once again snuggle under my covers like an ordinary girl, drifting off to sleep.*

Jolie and Carole relate more of their own early masturbatory sensations and experiences.

Jolie: *As I got older (elementary school age through high school), I started to do this in the comfort of my own bed, using pillows or bunched up blankets between my legs for friction. At this point, I did start to have fantasies—mostly about whoever was the big rock star or TV idol at the time. (As a baby boomer, I think Davy Jones of The Monkees got a lot of mileage!) The fantasies evolved from "stars" to real boys I knew once I hit middle school. As to other sensations, I remember accidentally rubbing against a desk at school and that feeling pretty good (though it would have been highly inappropriate to linger!).*

Carole: *When I was very young, not quite thirteen, I had not had any sex instruction at all. I was a little surprised at this new "experience" and felt puzzled as to what it was all about. I didn't have fantasies. I just closed my eyes and enjoyed the sensations. I can't remember any details, only that it felt delicious. Later, I loved heavy petting sessions with boyfriends. I remember them as being very wet and very enjoyable. The first time I had actual sex after all that petting, I found it to be a disappointment.*

Serena was very young when she first discovered she could give herself physical pleasure.

Serena: *I think I began touching myself when I was very young, certainly not older than ten or eleven. I was a bit of a lonely girl and was* *living in an isolated circumstance where I didn't have access to a lot of friends. To compensate, I made up a very vivid fantasy life, very rich and embroidered with details. I had one basic fantasy that I kept improving on time and time again. My fantasy definitely involved a boy, one that I only slightly knew and had very little actual contact with. I imagined myself in all kinds of situations with him, all very innocent now when I think about them, mostly about our being alone together and his arm or hand accidentally brushing against my arm or leg. I would touch myself between the legs while I indulged in my fantasy. I could spend hours doing this if I got the chance. Gradually, I built up my fantasy to full-fledged kissing where he pressed his lips against mine. I call these fantasies innocent because they never involved actual sex, which I knew nothing about anyway because I had no exposure and nobody spoke of things like that to me. But I experienced very voluptuous feelings in my masturbatory daydreams. I can say for sure that I frequently brought myself to orgasm, sometimes over and over again.*

Between pubescence and adolescence, many young goddesses or nymphs discover what feels good to them, as well as how to give themselves pleasure. But as they grow older and other people are introduced into the equation—real people, not fantasies—things begin to change. Think back to when you were a virgin but were beginning to have boyfriends or sexually precocious girlfriends. What kind of virginal orgasmic feelings did you experience when you were fooling around with them, necking or petting? What were your orgasmic experiences or pre-orgasmic sensations before you Did The Deed?

Agonizing Kissing

Some of the most essential and possibly sacramental sexual experiences for me occurred in a time period I've designated as the period of Virgin with Boyfriend. Virginal boyfriend sex, which I define as the activity of being more or less completely immersed for hours in agonizing kissing fits, was intense. Long periods of close physical proximity, mouth on mouth, the caressing of flesh, breathing in each other's air, often in close quarters (like a car or a closet), all that pent-up desire—there really is nothing like it! It's a pity more people who are not virgins anymore don't do it, because pre-intercourse sex is nothing more than extended foreplay. That means long kissing sessions, petting, snuggling, cuddling, fondling, mutual masturbation. Get back in touch with the sensations and feelings you experienced during this part of your sexual development, and you'll be well along your ultimate sex goddess odyssey.

Agonizing kissing is an essential element of virginal sex. The term "virginal sex" may sound like an oxymoron, but all sex goddesses understand the potency of the concept. I will never forget the hours spent rolling around on a bed with a boy I'll call K.S. His house was often empty in the afternoons even though he had two brothers. His mattress was hard and his bed king-sized. His room was angled to receive the most pleasant of afternoon light and was littered with the trappings of a teenage boy.

The aroma of his lightly soiled clothing possibly was an aphrodisiac to me. Another thing I remember about K.S. was that his skin was so smooth, almost as silky as a girl's. He had virtually no body hair, and the thick hair on his head was as shiny and black as an Asian's. His teeth were very white. In the half-light of a late April afternoon, they shone like pearls in his generous, liquid mouth with lips as plump as pink pillows. His lips were his chief charm, that and the fact that he was an amazing kisser. We spent hours lying in each other's arms kissing. Even though I knew he did not love me one whit (he did have another girlfriend), it mattered not, because his kisses sent me into delirium. His kisses produced multiple orgasms within me despite the fact that months went by before he touched so much as my breast.

The True Story of Annette and Caren

Another kissing story that occurred even earlier involved two of
my juvenile friends, who for privacy's sake I shall call Annette and
Caren, my nymph goddess seventh grade best friends. Annette had
bouncy shoulder length blond hair, sparkly brown eyes, and white,
nearly alabaster skin. Second oldest in a family of five kids,
Annette was a very hot-looking girl from a strict Catholic family. In
seventh grade, she seemed advanced to me because she shared a
room with her older sister who was allowed to date. Although
their mother set down rules about hemlines and makeup and her
older sister abided by them, Annette broke her mother's rules by
rolling her skirt up and applying mascara every day.

Caren came from a strong Lutheran background, but she managed to be a renegade any chance she got. She also had an older
sister who was dating. Annette and Caren were naturally curious,
which must have been the principle reason why we were drawn to
each other. I, too, was curious. But I was innocent as to what went
on between men and women because, unlike my friends, I did not
grow up in a traditional situation where parents were together and
where they could, undoubtedly, be heard making love. (Families
lived in smaller, less soundproof boxes in those days.) When you
are an adolescent and you are exposed to the sounds of sex, even
standard fare, garden variety, domesticated, middle-aged married
sex, your aural orgasmic energy is imprinted and becomes part of
your stimuli. The sounds your parents make when they are in bed
that seep through thin walls are forever hardwired into your sexual
circuitry. Even though you might be embarrassed by these sounds
when you are an adolescent and you realize what's going on, these
sounds of lovemaking stay with you forever and are part and
parcel of your sexual memory file.

Annette and Caren enjoyed practicing their kissing techniques
in preparation for a future day when they might have the oppor-

tunity to kiss boys. For many weeks, they practiced kissing their own reflections in hand mirrors, studying their expressions and experimenting with different things to do with their eyes. We three girls spent a fair amount of time in my mother's bedroom, seated at her vanity, trying on our kissing faces, and pressing our lips against the glass. Prerequisite to these kissing sessions was the trying on of my mother's makeup, a thrill for the other girls, whose mothers wore none. This is not to say that the other girls' mothers weren't attractive. But they did not project even the faintest whiff of sex goddessness. By comparison, my mother was Nefertiti, with her eyelash curler and her sooty box of cake eyeliner that came with its own miniature wand. Once the makeup was on, it wasn't long before Annette and Caren fell to kissing each other, intuiting even as budding nymph goddesses that practice makes perfect in preparation for the real thing. But the danger (if it was a danger) of permitting lip to press lip at one point overwhelmed them. They were deep into a practice session one day when the unthinkable happened. Annette slapped Caren. Why? Because Caren's body had gone to mush, and in a trance-like state she had become aroused and was unconsciously grinding her pelvis against Annette's. What happened was involuntary. What passed between them was an electricity so profound that it produced a response in Annette and certainly one in Caren, who had been doing the grinding.

A Young Girl's First Orgasm

Roxanne remembers her virginal erotic encounters with her high school boyfriend, Jack, and her first orgasm.

Roxanne: *I was a senior in high school and in love with Jack, who was a year older than me. We hadn't had sex, but were both madly in lust. One night, while lying on the family room floor behind my mom's blue*

*recliner, we were at it hot and heavy with only a minor amount of fully
clothed bodies rubbing together, when all of a sudden I had these delightful and overpowering spasms. At first I was completely unaware what
was going on, but as they continued, I figured out I was having an
orgasm and just let it all go. I told Jack, of course, who was totally into
the concept—totally!—so much so that we proceeded to have oral sex for
the first time because he wanted to feel me come in his mouth. It gives
me the shivers just talking about it. We had a passionate relationship!*

More First Orgasm Stories
from Former Virgins

Her first orgasm with a boyfriend brought on by a kissing fit led
Jolie into experimenting with other pleasures of sex.

Jolie: *I think the idea of "agonizing kissing" is dead-on. What was
exciting for me about my sexual growth with a partner was meeting all
the benchmarks—the light kissing which led to the more passionate kissing (and French kissing); the touching over the clothes, touching in
underwear, and then touching naked; licking and sucking of various
body parts (breasts/nipples, belly button, pubic area, etc.). As I explored
further and further, I recall the whole evolution being amazingly erotic—
a big point of no return, because now I was experiencing the real thing
and not just fantasizing about doing it anymore.*

Jane still thinks agonizing kissing is orgasm-inducing hot.

Jane: *In my pre-sex days, I think kissing was the biggest deal. (Even in
the prime of my life, I'd still rather have great kissing than anything,
because without it, the rest is not as hot.) It went on for hours and
hours until my lips were raw. I would get all these little quivers and
throbs inside and outside my vagina. I would never have officially called
them "orgasms," but in retrospect, I suppose they were, though not the
powerful, full-fledged kind I'd get from consummating the sex act.*

Virgins Can and Do Engage in Oral Sex

It used to be that oral sex was something couples explored after they'd had intercourse. Today, oral sex is considered to be simply another form of intimacy, one that does not necessarily preclude or come after standard intercourse. For a female, receiving oral sex, i.e., having someone "go down" on her, can be an explosive and thoroughly pleasurable orgasmic experience that she can enjoy while leaving her hymen intact and maintaining her virginity.

Riva was a virgin when she had her first orgasm via receiving oral sex.

Riva: *My high school boyfriend, M., who was my first love, was an amazing lover—focused, attentive, never in a rush. He was a great kisser and gave all of himself in our "heavy petting" sessions, which lasted hours and hours. The two things I remember most (and I still remember after all this time) was how he kissed my breasts, which drove me wild, and the time we were using his older sister's house when she was out of town. He performed oral sex on me for the first time. I was so taken aback by this, I was immobilized, but I do recall the experience being rather amazing. I didn't climax at that time, but I was so ready and willing to have sexual intercourse with him, I was out of my mind! We didn't do that yet, but came close. The other thing that drove me wild was being naked in bed with him and feeling his erect penis circling my crotch and vaginal opening—talk about willpower! We had decided we weren't yet ready to have sex, but played around dangerously like this. He actually inserted himself into me about a inch or two then quickly pulled out. That was also very intense.*

A Virgin Orgasm Explodes out of an Adolescent Game

From my own personal point of reference, one of the most intense nymph goddess experiences I enjoyed one summer on an ongoing basis had to do with chicken fights. Yes, chicken fights! That's the game young teens play in a pool or the ocean where a girl climbs on a boy's shoulders and another girl does the same thing and then the two try to knock each other off their male mount. I was twelve or thirteen, certainly at the beginning of my adolescence. A group of boys and girls hung out at the beach every day, too young to work, too old to stay close to home.

Adolescents have a natural urge to be close to one another. Their bodies are caught up in a tide of hormonal change. They naturally play pre-mating games, which is why they love sitting on each other's laps, bumping into each other, mock-wrestling, and tickling. As it was, so much oiled and tanned flesh and the skimpiness of our bathing apparel caused a constant state of low-grade arousal to be in force at all times. Heading for the water, was, I think, an instinct to cool off.

But I was anything but cooled off astride the broad shoulders of my usual chicken-fight partner, an unusually well-built young man named Frank. The odd thing was I didn't like Frank very much, but we functioned superbly as a team. On top of him, like a mino-taur, I could easily defeat girls twice my size. It could have been the fury of the fight or the waves knocking against me or simply the pressure generated from my entire bottom straddling his muscular young neck as he gripped my thighs to keep me from tumbling, but in any case, the first orgasm I actually remember experiencing came from those chicken fights. The sensation of my climax was so profound, so intense, that I uncharacteristically lost my balance and toppled into the sea. The cold water closing over my head revived me perhaps more quickly than I wished. I remember being flustered and feeling embarrassed, even though no one else seemed to notice anything, except for Frank, naturally, who later up on the beach commented I'd been squeezing his neck pretty hard. I blushed and turned away from him, and for a few days, declined to participate in the game.

The Fantasy of Surrender,
or Being "Overwhelmed"

One recurring sexual fantasy leading to orgasm often begins in virginal adolescence—the desire to be "forced" into doing something you wanted to do anyway. The sexual fantasy of surrender, the desire to "let go," to give yourself over to another authority, is awesome and powerful. Here's what Jane had to say:

Jane: *Occasionally, my early teenage fantasies involved some form of mild bondage. Growing up in more conservative times, I had a lot of guilt about my own pleasure. The only way to compensate was to fantasize that I had to be coaxed or coerced into sex, putting the "blame," so to speak, on my partner rather than on myself. But my craving for pleasure was always too strong to be denied. So there were times alone in my room when I prepared myself for a bout of masturbation by tying a blindfold on myself.*

One Man's Opinion

Jake is very familiar with the "I want to be taken" fantasy.

Jake: *Most women at some point in their lives entertain some version of a rape fantasy. It happens mostly in the woman's late adolescence, or that's been my experience. Of course, they want to be "taken" by a handsome romance book guy who really loves them, but that's part of the fantasy. Sometimes the fantasy lasts for years. I try to accommodate these whims of my various girlfriends when they arise.*

Virgins Want to Know

Did I Have an Orgasm or Not?

A question young goddesses occasionally ask themselves is, "Did I have an orgasm or not?" Some women describe their adolescent experiences with orgasm as more of a rippling, tingling sensation, not necessarily one big climactic release. Many adult women experience this kind of long-lasting lower grade stimulation as more pleasing than one big blast that is quickly over. But since even young, virginal females are physiologically capable of sustained multiorgasmic sensations, who's to say what is best?

Riva's juvenile masturbatory experiences gave her insight into what pleasures her as an adult.

Riva: *I always climaxed from my early masturbatory episodes and later from heavy petting sessions. In retrospect, I see how helpful they were to be orgasmic as an adult. I was not only comfortable "letting go" with myself, but some of the techniques—experimenting with whether I liked constant pressure on my clitoris while masturbating, or enhancing my pleasure by pinching my nipples a little bit while I touched myself between my legs—whatever I enjoyed doing to myself, I have been able to transfer to use with a partner, enabling me to have an orgasm during intercourse, which I know is difficult for a lot of women.*

Tips for Virgin Goddesses

Learn to ride a horse. Practice posting.

Cultivate a richly erotic daydream life.

Practice bringing yourself to a state of high arousal without ever touching yourself.

Develop a crush on a movie star or other exciting-to-you idol (it could be the person who sits next to you in class) and construct an erotic fantasy around them to encourage you to masturbate.

Learn to give yourself pleasure in a myriad of ways. Don't get hung up on one self-pleasuring routine. Experiment.

Primping and Preparation

Sexy Tip: Practice parading around the house in your underwear. Get used to the way you look and feel wearing it. Don't just tug it on and quickly cover it up! Practice modeling your underwear in front of a mirror.

---

*T*here are a few simple rules for dressing for Goddessex. You don't have to own a garter belt, a bustier, or a pair of crotchless panties. You don't even have to own a thong, even though thongs are the hottest selling undergarment in the universe. If these undergarments already own pride of place in your lingerie drawer, that's wonderful. Go to the head of the class! But it's not necessary to dress the part of a tart or a strumpet to feel like a sexy goddess.

Yes, Your Underwear Does Matter

Let's start with brassieres. My friend Roxanne attests that changing her bras literally changed her life. Her transformation began when she complained to me about the sorry state of her sex life. According to Roxanne, all her underwear was strictly "anything cotton, anything practical, anything I can throw in the washing machine." I called her on the carpet when she admitted that comfort was her only criterion. I have nothing against comfort. Who feels sexy in underwear that chafes or binds?

Fortunately, there is a great deal of beautiful underwear that is a pleasure to wear. Wacoal, Rampage, Felina, Jezebel, Aubade, even Maidenform make beautiful, enticing, uber-feminine garments.

Look for sensual, even decadent fabrics. Satin, silk, fishnet, and lace feel amazing against the skin. Uh-oh, you say. I have no inclination to handwash! Not a problem. All but the most fragile lingerie can be run through the washing machine on the delicate cycle using a lingerie bag.

Find Your Correct Size

The first challenge in buying a sexy bra is finding your correct size. According to major bra manufacturers, most women are incorrectly bra-ed. Mostly, their bras are too small. Their custom is to buy a size they've bought many times before, even before childbirth, or close their eyes to the fact that their bra doesn't fit. They assume their partners aren't looking either. And it's true that some don't.

The consequences of wearing an incorrectly sized bra is that the back rides up, your breasts spill unflatteringly out of the cups, and you can develop permanent grooves on your shoulders from where the straps dig in. Not only do you look awful, but you're uncomfortable, which can make you feel insecure and vulnerable. You want to feel good, even powerful in your underwear. It is your goddess armor!

Your first goddess directive is to hie thee to a good department store or intimate wear specialty shop to be fitted by a trained salesperson. Most women have never had the experience of being properly measured and fitted for a bra, which can be done at any good lingerie store. The chain store Victoria's Secret offers personal fitting. Once you know your right size, you can have fun shopping.

Bras and Panties Should Match

The rule of thumb is that if you're buying a new bra, buy the panties that go with it. It doesn't matter what style of panties you prefer. Bikini, boycut, briefs, string, even the thong are all good as long as you feel good wearing them. I have my personal favorites—I tend to go for anything black, and I like my bras décolleté—but if you adore color, go for it. I find it very inspiring to open my lingerie drawer in the morning to see a nice stack of matching bras and panties. Even if nobody sees your underwear but you, you'll find that even on the most drudgy, low-energy days, you'll feel upbeat and sexy the minute you begin getting dressed. If you have a lover, invite input. Be aware that it can be tragically disappointing, however, if you discover your partner doesn't share your enthusiasm for attractive matching lingerie, or worse, doesn't even notice. Shane was terrifically disappointed.

Shane: *My first husband noticed nothing about my lingerie. Nothing. I used to think it was great that he noticed nothing, because I thought it made him easy to please. I remember being somewhat disappointed when we first started going out and I realized he didn't care about my underwear, because I had kick-ass underwear. I had lots of sexy bras and panties from my job in the fashion industry when I was being exposed to all kinds of terrific stuff. It was kind of a hobby of mine to collect it. He didn't care about it in the least. That upset me somewhat. Eventually, I realized he didn't care about my underwear because he just wanted to have sex with me, and underwear, in his opinion, only got in the way. That wasn't what I wanted. I wanted a lover who was playful about sexy underthings, who could share my enthusiasm for self-adornment, who, let's face it, actually looked at me. That's why he became my "first husband."*

Try Wearing Your Bra in Bed

You might have noticed how, in some of the racier cable TV shows, women tend to leave their bras on when they're in bed with their lovers. That's due in part to clauses in their contracts some actresses have about actual nudity. The fact is, wearing bras in bed is sexy.

Why? Because a totally naked body is only half as alluring as a partially clothed one. A major rule of Goddessex is that you should always leave something on, even if it's only your pearls.

Do leave your bra on, especially if you're planning on riding your partner. Imagine yourself astride, as though you are riding a horse. You're wearing your best bra. Your partner gets the image of your glowing, polished flesh juxtaposed against smooth satin or a froth of lace. Your breasts are lifted and held by delicate feminine garments, presented like a beautiful offering. It's a very sexy gesture to lift your breasts from the cups so that your partner can suckle your nipples or tease them with his lips or fingertips. Leaving the bra on can also enhance your breasts, making them look better than they might in their unadorned, totally natural state. Imagine for a moment how much more appetizing garnished food looks than something served plain on the plate. Your pleasure in eating is enhanced because of the lovely presentation.

Bras are a big deal, and talking underwear is a natural prerogative for modern goddesses. For example, in 1997, *People* magazine voted the New York State Westchester County District Attorney Jeannine Pirro one of their "50 Most Beautiful People in the World." Pirro, who in 2003 authored the book *To Punish and Protect*, told *More* magazine all about her underwear fetish and how she loves LaPerla bras. The lady has good taste! I love LePerla and LeJaby. They are a bit pricey, but worth their weight in gold to any woman aspiring to be a sex goddess. Of course, you don't have to spend a fortune in lingerie to have a great orgasm, but if beautiful underthings make you feel sexy and attractive, why would you not?

Try a Total "About Face" and Skip the Bra Sometimes

As wonderful as bras are, don't wear one every day. There is the issue of support to consider (if you are very heavy-breasted or pregnant or nursing, you probably always wear a bra to bed whether you think it's sexy or not), but for your own self-awareness sensuality education purposes, you need to experience going braless at least once in a while. Try doing it on a weekend or even walking around your house if your job makes not wearing a bra nearly impossible.

The point of going braless once in a while is to become more familiar with your breasts, specifically your nipples. Your breasts are two of your most major erogenous zones. Your nipples are mostly erectile tissue, filled with sensation. You want to fully experience how your nipples respond to being cold or in close proximity to someone you find attractive. If you wear a bra all the time, you become disassociated from parts of your own body. Your breasts are capable of responding to all kinds of stimuli. Cold, scent, physical activity, the way your bare nipples feel rubbing against your clothing, how they respond to another person's sexual energy are all exciting things to experience. You've got to let the puppies out of the pen sometimes!

A Few Words About Panties

Here are a few good things to consider about what you're wearing on the bottom. And when not to wear anything.

- White, black, coral, or turquoise, whatever color panties you choose, the usual rule is they should match your bra for a polished presentation. Unless you always wear black panties. Black panties look good with everything.
- Leave your panties on as long as possible. The revealing of your vagina should be treated as a gift. Don't be too hasty in removing the wrapping paper.
- Even if it looks sexy in an adult movie, it's not sensible to leave your panties on during sex. You can leave them on and

have your partner enter you through a leg hole with the crotch of the panties pulled aside. But while stunts like this do lend an element of surprise (and possibly unnecessary challenges) to making love, be prepared that your favorite panties are quite likely to get ripped. That can get very expensive. Only make a habit of this trick if you have a lover who loves buying you panties.

- Likewise, eschew panties once in a while. Keep a diary of your random thoughts and impressions as you go about the day pantyless. Your near-naked state, even under all the rest of your clothes, will help you understand what turns you on. Without that extra layer of material, no matter how fine or gossamer the weave, you will more easily recognize the things that mildly arouse or stimulate you. It could be that vanilla candle you sniffed in an aromatherapy shop or the hard, masculine scent of leather in a men's furnishing store.

Your Lingerie Must-Have List

Roxanne, who has graduated from utilitarian underwear to become a bona fide and self-described Lingerie Monster, provided this list of her must-have underpinnings.

"Nothing trumps the total sexiness of a well-fitting white cotton/microfiber bra. Sexy does *not* need to be frilly! Fit is everything. The following are must-haves for me, at least:

Underwire camisoles in black, nude, and white.

Four underwire bras, seamless, no frills, in white, black, and nude, plus One Fun Color (this season it's turquoise), with panties to match.

Several bras just for fun: a front-hook black "balcony" bra and a great demi-cup push-up bra with removable pads . . . absolutely necessary when you're in the mood to play "tart."

Two one-piece sleek and smooth teddies with a snap-closure
crotch.

For those on a strict budget, nix anything white. Black is a basic,
but nude can substitute for white.

To Roxanne's list, I'd like to add a few must-haves of my own: One
sexy nightgown. One pair of regular hose and a garter belt. One
push-up bra. And, yes, it should be half padded even if you think
you have padding to spare. Try one on and you'll see why padding
in the lower half of the cup is an asset even to the most full-
bosomed body.

Setting the Stage: Your Bedroom

**Sexy Tip: If your bed is a four-poster, try hanging
white Christmas lights all around the top. Not
only is it festive (even in July), but those little
white lights are the ultimate in inexpensive sexy
lighting!**

From this moment forward, you will no longer refer to the room
that you sleep/make love/pleasure yourself in as the "bedroom."
Think of it as your "boudoir," which is French for a woman's bed-
or dressing room. The word "boudoir" automatically confers a
more sensual image. The sooner you begin regarding this special
room as your personal love chamber, the sooner you will begin
having more orgasmic pleasure in it.

Accoutrements

Before opening a discussion as to what you should (or should
not) have in your boudoir, you must address the primary issue:
Do you share it? Notice I didn't ask if you were sharing your

boudoir with a "god" or "consort" or even "fellow goddess," although in the best possible scenario, you will be playing hostess with the mostest to a person who loosely fits those descriptions. Whether or not you live alone or share your boudoir on a regular or irregular basis, the aesthetic choices you make should totally please *you*. Your bedroom/boudoir is your personal stage and theater where many of your most intimate and thrilling romances and dramas will happen. Some of the elements to consider in decorating and furnishing this room include sheets, lighting, and the bed itself. There are also accessories you might have, things that add a special ambience, such as candles or an incense holder, artwork, books, flowers, basically anything you like to keep on your night table.

Some goddesses, especially married ones, choose to go for what's sexy but traditional.

Betsy: *Our (notice I didn't say "my") bedroom is a delightful sherbet lemon-lime color, with long white sheer curtains on black wrought-iron rods. Our bed is queen-sized. It's black and has what furniture mavens and interior decorators call a high pencil-post frame. It's sexy, but simple. I've arranged the bed to look out a window onto a beautiful view that features our favorite ash tree, which is more than 150 years old. The room has a beautiful armoire and two antique bureaus. The bed has a white-and-black toile duvet and big matching pillows. Next to my bed, I keep a Tiffany clock that we received as a wedding gift. I keep three amethyst stones for good luck and good vibes on the night table. Our room is refreshing, well-lit, quietly colorful, and definitely striving for simplicity in design. And if the walls could talk. . .*

Alec, a single man, put in his two cents about feminine lairs. What's sexy to him is a variety of things. He's not hung up on any one boudoir look, other than to say that "a few stuffed animals on the bed is fine. More than a few makes me think she might be a bit strange." Alec "gets around." He's been a private guest in a large number of female bedrooms. He volunteered that he "loves to see bits and pieces of sexy lingerie lying around." He also feels more at ease if the woman's room is a bit messy. "I don't mind seeing a bit of soiled underwear on the floor. It's humanizing." A sexy woman with whom he shared a multi-orgasmic night left a scrap of expensive silk lingerie hanging on the doorknob of her bathroom. "I just saw that pink silk and I wanted to sniff it." A woman who is too neat frankly freaks him out. "If she gets too hung up about stuff getting on her precious bedspread, I'm outta there. How can anybody enjoy themselves if they're too hung up on making a mess?"

Roxanne says she is "totally bedroom picky. Totally! I don't know if it's sexy to anyone or not, but I keep it the way I need it to be." Here are some of her specifics.

Roxanne: *My sheets are 100 percent cotton only—Wamsutta "twill" sateen sheets. I have only a fitted sheet over a very thick mattress pad. I also have a down duvet with either a flannel cover or a great high thread count cotton cover, depending on the season. My sheets are white, and the duvet cover is natural/ecru/ivory. I tried patterned sheets once, but they didn't feel calming to me.*

Subdued Lighting Is Essential

Lighting is another essential element to creating the perfect boudoir. Lighting can make or break a mood. Again, Roxanne was specific.

Roxanne: *No overhead lights are allowed in my bedroom, ever. Period. I have a ceiling fan and will not attach lights to it. I have two lamps in my room, one that a former lover fitted for me. It's an original Mission lantern that's all rusty and has white art glass. He redid the wiring and put on a cord with a switch. It's on my great-grandfather's Victorian* *oak dresser on top of a white linen cloth. I love it! I also have a small lamp on my bedside table, which is an old board on top of my radiator. The lamp has a rusty finish on the metal and is very streamlined. The shade is wicker, and I also love that!*

Your Bed Is Your Stage

If your boudoir is the theater, your bed is the actual stage. This is the place where your most memorable orgasms will probably happen. There are some very sexy beds out there. Four-poster. Old-fashioned iron. Mission beds. Sleigh beds. Platform beds. The European Flou bed, which is a kind of platform bed. Even Murphy beds (the kind that open out of a closet) can be exciting. But just remember this: goddesses never sleep on futons laid flat on the floor, and sofa beds are a complete no-no except for the occasional overnight guest. As Alec put it, "The bed itself doesn't really matter that much. The important thing is that it's an inviting space." Another single man likes that every woman's bedroom reveals something personal about that woman.

Mack: *I don't care and don't notice that much about a woman's bedroom, although each woman's bedroom is different and each tells a story about that woman. A guy should always be aware that a woman's bedroom is really her private little haven. And that it's a privilege for him to be there.*

He offered his illuminating observations about female bedrooms.

Mack: *Sometimes the more successful in her career the woman is, the more childlike her bedroom. You'd be surprised how many high-powered women have dolls on their beds, lots of stuffed animals. That can be a turn-on, because it reflects an image so different from her daytime life. Some women have really lavish bedrooms that are all done up like their personal stage sets. That can be very exciting, because it means she's* *invited you to play opposite her on that stage. But I also really dig it when a woman's bedroom is messy. As long as it's not filthy, I don't mind a little bit of dirt. It's sexy to me, actually. It turns me on that she's a little bit indifferent about how she presents herself, that she doesn't care all that much. It makes me nervous if the room's too perfect, if she's got the candles lit in advance, everything arranged, music, chilled champagne on the night table, everything planned out. I like to think that what's happening between us is more spontaneous. It's weird when every detail of the seduction chamber has been totally planned.*

Glenn also doesn't mind a woman who is a bit messy.

Glenn: *At the end of the day, it depends on the woman. If the woman can pull off the unmade bed and the dresser drawers hanging open, there's something admirable about that. A dirty goddess is really sexy, but her dirtiness cannot offend my concept of femininity. I guess what I mean is I don't like real dirt. I like a woman whose body is totally clean, but her room can be a bit disheveled or unkempt. It means she's a bit loose, willing to let her hair get mussed.*

C., my special muse whose experience and wisdom guided me throughout this book, offered his astute observations on the vagaries of different goddesses' private chambers. Some of what he had to say might strike readers as painful, but I think they are important tidbits. Here's what C. said.

C: *The Married Woman's bedroom never changes. It's neither perfect nor messy. If something's off about the married woman's sex life (which it must be, if she's invited me into her bed), it's usually because of the boredom factor. My suggestion to the woman who finds herself in this rut is to stir things up. She can start with fresh props. She should buy a wig that's completely different from her hair and leave it on the bedpost. If not a wig, a riding helmet or a riding crop. Her husband might be startled when she comes on to him in bed with a wig on, but here's the*

*thing: Men are a little slow. A woman's got to kick-start a guy's imagi-
nation to get him fired up. She can leave a sexy magazine around, even
a catalogue like Victoria's Secret. Once she gets him revved up, he'll get
the idea, and then she won't need a guy like me to make her happy. If
she's otherwise happily married, that's a good thing.*

*The Divorced Woman's bedroom is another story. It's always . . . perfect.
She's got the big down comforter, and her curtains are color-coordinated
to perfectly match her duvet. Everything looks so . . . ready. The entire
atmosphere screams "expectant," which matches the woman's psycho-
logical state. I always feel a bit badly for divorced women when I get into
their bedrooms. They appreciate every little bullshit thing you do for
them. Making love to them sometimes is like throwing food to the
hungry. Most of the divorced women I've been with were married to
total dickheads. They're usually forty or fifty years old. A lot of them
are still in their beautiful homes with their beautiful bedrooms, everything so carefully picked out. Their husbands ditched them because they
wanted a younger woman or became obsessed with the idea of a ménage.
The guy's wife is still beautiful, but he doesn't want her anymore. That's
why they encourage younger men. I try my best to please them, but sometimes they're happiest left alone with their vibrators. Sometimes they
have quite the collection. You open the drawer of their night tables and
some of them have a real arsenal.*

Jamie, a divorced goddess, had this to say about her private space.

Jamie: *I think one of the reasons I'm so totally into my bedroom is
because in the two years I was married, my husband never finished a
bedroom for "us." It was a meaningless concept to him. We slept in a
room that was never painted, it was never calming, it was never really
clean. I am so thrilled to have my own room. In fact, if I ever remarry
I will insist on a room of my own. Not for sleeping (because I am planning on great sex and cuddling!), but because I now appreciate the joy
of my own space.*

My muse confided a little-known secret. Guys really like all that girly stuff.

C.: *It's really nice to be in a totally feminine environment. Guys really love a frilly and feminine bed. They can't make their own beds really nice like that because it would be considered strange. Unless a man is really insecure about his masculinity, it's a rush to make love to a woman and then loll around with her afterward in her smooth, silky bed. Usually, all her girly stuff gets me excited and I want to make love to her again and give her another orgasm.*

TV or No TV?

Will you have a television in your bedroom or not? I am of two minds on this subject. Having a TV/VCR in the bedroom means you can enjoy erotic movies with or without a friend. But if you watch TV in bed before falling asleep, you're less likely to make love. But you might be a woman whose orgasm is enhanced by keeping your eyes trained on something exciting on the screen while your partner is working on you. If this is true for you, I say, "Go for it!"

A Few Domestic Goddess Words of Advice

- Flannel sheets in the winter are sexy. Why? Because the bed is warm when you hop in it! Plus, flannel picks up moisture . . . all kinds.
- Keeping a few candles by the bed is nice. Everybody looks more attractive in candlelight. Don't forget to extinguish the flame when your flames have expired. All your post-orgasm pleasure will be spoiled if you wind up your evening with a call to the fire department!
- You might adore the look of white linens, but unless you're either olive-skinned or have a tan, alabaster skin is not

enhanced by white sheets. As an interior designer friend once told a client, "Go for ecru, darling. With your pale skin, on white sheets you'll look like a corpse."

- A goddess can never have too many pillows. Pillows are feminine, soft; you can put them under your bottom or rest your elbows on them to cushion yourself in certain sexual positions. Trust me, sex is better with pillows. After your orgasm, as you recover from a passionate love bout, the two of you can prop your heads on them for a little pillow talk.

The Goddess Orgasm Diet: What Does a Sex Goddess Eat?

Sexy Tip: Don't eat or feed your lover asparagus for a full day before making love.

---

*T*here are a million diets out there promising to help you lose weight, increase your stamina, manage your allergies, lower your cholesterol, boost your calcium, or reduce the risk of heart attack. Not a single one of them promises to give you orgasms. Are you surprised? That's because there is no specific diet—yet— that will give you more orgasms. I would be going out on a limb to claim that any special diet or one particular food that you can go out of your way to eat is going to bring you to exquisite climax. I do know many women who say that slowly nibbling away at one of their food favorites (fudge is one example) is just as satisfying to them as having an orgasm. Personally, wrapping my lips around an enormous Italian combo submarine sandwich does it for me. Of course, it has to be from The White House, a world-famous eatery on Arctic Avenue in Atlantic City, New Jersey, especially when I can wash it down with sips of ice-cold Dr. Pepper. I would be hard pressed to say which experience is more pleasurable— devouring one of those amazing sandwiches or being devoured all afternoon in bed by a talented lover. Hmmm, maybe both the lover and the sandwich . . . now that's multiorgasmic!

You Are What You Eat

If your sexual response seems diminished, consider your daily diet. There is much truth to the old saying, "You are what you eat." In the great days of ancient mythology, when Psyche and Indra— Greek and Eastern Indian goddesses, respectively—weren't casting spells, moving mountains, or delivering justice, they lolled around nibbling sweet almonds and grapes. According to mythology, only the daintiest, most aphrodisiacal food crossed their goddess lips. If you read enough stories, it appears that the goddesses breakfasted on morning dew, lapped peach nectar in the afternoon, and ended their day sucking on figs and pomegranates.

Unless you are living the life of a modern Psyche, chances are you're not putting perfect food in your mouth. If you're breakfasting on donuts and making your evening meal a jar of olives, correct this at once. Begin by saying to yourself, "I will not put food that is not good for me into my mouth." Once you start the process of truly regarding your body as a temple, you will have an easier time choosing whether to nourish it or defile it.

You already know which foods are doing you no good. Place a goddess curse on your dependence on them right now. Break the bagel habit! Many women make the mistake of soothing themselves with food. Calories will make you warm (a calorie is a unit of heat) but an excess of food gratification will not make your sex life better and eventually it will make you fat.

Vary Your Diet

Other foods should be enjoyed but eaten in moderation. These would include sour cream, butter, any of the fats. Some fats—especially those contaning omega-3 fatty acids—are actually quite good for you (many nuts and certainly olive oil are prime examples), but that doesn't mean you should make an entire meal of them.

It's also a good idea to eat different things every day and not fall into a routine where you always have a container of yogurt for lunch, even though yogurt is good for you. The Diabetes Online Reference Web site offers evidence that eating the same food— even good food—every day increases your risk of developing Type II diabetes. Repetition of the same foods every day stimulates the body to make excessive insulin, which can trigger the disease. The right diet for women over forty is the one doctors have dubbed the "Rainbow Diet" for its emphasis on brightly colored vegetables and fruits.

What to Eat

There is a lot to be said for sensual pleasures of "mouth feel," but an excess of food gratification will not make your sex life better. There are many wonderful things to put in your mouth besides cheesecake. Pledge to banish really bad food from your life right now. Fried food. Fast food. Anything (other than caviar!) that's loaded with salt. Avoid dosing yourself with sugar. Drink water, not soda. Avoid processed food or anything boasting a long shelf life, like Pop Tarts or any of those cellophane-wrapped snacks and cupcakes. They're stuffed with preservatives, not to mention empty calories. The foods I'm going to mention here are known as aphrodisiacs. What is an aphrodisiac? It's something that supposedly makes you feel sexy or puts you "in the mood" for sex. The following foods are considered to be aphrodisiacs because they have a sensual feel or taste or because they are rich in vitamins or protein or, as in the case of chocolate, contain chemicals known to actually trigger the libido portion of the brain. In any case, enjoy all of the following foods, albeit in moderation. Too much of anything will make you feel either overfed or sick. In other words, they're not conducive to your optimal sexual experience.

Oysters Are More Than a Good Source of Protein

While no one food source is a guarantee for orgasm, some foods are more inspiring than others. There are foods that you can enjoy that truly will enhance your sexual experiences. Oysters, for example, are not called the "food of love" for nothing. Oysters are pure protein. They are an energy booster that, unlike pasta, won't leave you feeling stuffed. Plus, just ordering them in a restaurant is tantamount to sending your lover a message that you're in the mood for love. Oysters are undeniably associated in the public mind with horniness. Because they are so reputed to be a sexy food, many fine restaurants offer them on their Valentine's Day specials. Served on the half shell, they slide down your throat in one wet glob, sort of like something else that later might be sliding down that very channel. Rumor and reputation notwithstanding, oysters honestly are a food for love, because they contain high levels of zinc. Zinc has been clinically proven to improve the sex drive. Sexually speaking, zinc doesn't just benefit women. Male porn stars—professional studs—take zinc every day.

Fish Eggs Are Good for You

Another well-documented food for love are the eggs of the sturgeon, better known as caviar. They contain large amounts of the vitamins A, D, B1, B2, and B6, as well as phosphorous. These vitamins and the mineral phosphorous are stimulants to the circulatory system. Your circulation is integral to your orgasm, because in order to become fully aroused, blood must be able to quickly rush to the significant portions of your anatomy. You could just go to the health food store and stock up on vitamin pills, but if you enjoy the experience of eating caviar and the whole production around it (chopped egg, chopped onion, melba toast rounds, or toast points), it's much more fun to take your vitamins that way. A flute of champagne on the side can't hurt. A little bit of alcohol is a stimulant; a lot is not.

Celery Is More Than a Diet Food

You thought celery was a diet food just because it contains zero calories. Celery, however, enjoys a reputation for being an aphrodisiac. In ancient times, it was rumored to be a food for love. Rich in the vitamins A, C, and B and potassium, celery also contains loads of minerals. The seeds of the stalky growth are also said to be an aphrodisiac.

Chocolate Tastes Great and It's Good for You, Too

There are certain foods that enjoy a reputation as an enhancement to orgasm. Chocolate was actually banned from monasteries years ago because of its sexy reputation. Chocolate *is* sexy. It contains small traces of caffeine, which is a stimulant. Another mild stimulant, theobromine, is also present in chocolate in slightly higher amounts. Phenylethylamine, of the amphetamine family, is also a chemical component found in chocolate. Possibly, it is the combination of the three that explains the "lift" chocolate eaters experience when they nibble their favorite chocolate treats. Theories abound as to why eating chocolate makes us feel sexier. The most controversial one emerged from researchers at the Neurosciences Institute in San Diego, who say that chocolate contains pharmacologically active substances that have a similar effect on the brain to marijuana. These chemicals may be the ones responsible for certain drug-induced psychoses associated with chocolate craving. Chocolate, they say, doesn't exactly make you high, but certain compounds it contains may account for that warm and fuzzy feeling so many of us experience when we eat it. Finally, chocolate relaxes us and lowers inhibitions. It may be the perfect sex food!

Figs Resemble Your Vagina

Eat fresh green figs, not dried. They were enjoyed by the ancient
Greeks as a prelude to their sex orgies. I love a fresh fig dripping
with nectar, but they are very lush so one is usually enough. A
split-open fresh fig greatly resembles the female vulva (the fruit
inside is pussy pink), which is another reason it is discussed when
sex is on the mind.

Radishes Aren't Just a Garnish

Used primarily as a garnish in our culture, radishes are seldom
eaten and are often tossed away; the Egyptian pharaohs, however,
considered radishes to be nothing short of divine. Was it because of
their semen-y tangy taste or something else about them? Good sex
requires plenty of energy, and raw vegetables possess more vitamins
and minerals than cooked food. Besides, radishes contain plenty of
vitamins A, B, and D, which are considered to be aphrodisiacal.

Almonds and Vanilla Inspire the Olfactory System

These flavors smell good both separately and together, and
almonds and vanilla act as pheromones on the olfactory system.
Pheromones, by the way, are the olfactory component, however
subtle, that make one person attractive to another. Almonds are
really good for you as well: they are on many of the antioxidant
diets.

Truffles Are Musky

The mushrooms—not the candy—are considered a sexy food
because of their rarity and because of what many women find to
be their sexy, musky, masculine odor. They cost the earth, which
for some women automatically makes them a stimulant!

And Don't Forget . . .

Other orgasm-friendly foods include avocados, walnuts (some cultures toss walnuts at newlyweds as a way of wishing fertility on them), and honey. Your vaginal secretions will be more fresh and delicious if you make a habit of snacking on watermelon. The juice is not only loaded with antioxidants, but it perfumes the system, leaving your lady juices mild and sweet.

A Special Word About Asparagus

Are there any foods an orgasm goddess should specifically avoid eating within an hour or so of making love? Yes. Asparagus. Asparagus makes your juices smell bad. It turns your urine dark brown as well. If you're thinking of bestowing the gift of oral sex on your male partner, don't feed him asparagus for dinner. It will turn his semen positively rank. If you're one of those goddesses who is not crazy about swallowing semen anyway, you'll be even less likely to do it if your lover suddenly develops a craving for this vegetable. This doesn't mean you should stop eating it. Asparagus is good for you—chockablock full of vitamins, minerals, and other things that your body needs. Plus it looks kind of sexy when a woman picks up the spears and eats them with her fingers. So eat asparagus in abundance—just not before making love!

PART II

Immersing Yourself in Sensuality

Think of yourself as a free-floating entity of sexual desire.

—Goddess motto

Getting in Touch with Your Inner Sensualist

$\mathcal{W}$hen your alarm clock goes off in the morning (and isn't that tiresome? Did the original goddesses have to endure alarms clocks?), the first thing on your mind might not be how you can fulfill your sex goddess destiny. But it should be. You're thinking, "Dog must go out, must pull kids' lunches together, is it my turn to go out and warm up the car?" Modern goddesses, unfortunately, have to concern themselves with such things. Boo hoo. It's just a sad twist of fate that unless you happen to be very wealthy (in the most material sense of the word), you probably don't have any acolytes (er, servants) to perform these irksome tasks for you. But that doesn't mean you can't or shouldn't take a few moments every single day to nourish your goddessness. Here's how to begin.

Stretch and Stroke: Goddess Exercises

Every goddess needs an exercise regimen—make this one yours! You don't even have to get up to do these exercises. Begin your stretching/stroking routine before you leave the bed. It's very nice if you can do your routine on fresh clean sheets that have been air-dried in the sun. In appropriate weather, mine are. But if your sheets won't fit this description, don't let it throw you. Stains and rumpled sheets are a fact of life, not a deterrent to inner happiness.

The purpose of the bed stretch is to return your body to its natural sensual state. I hear some naysayers protesting that they are already annoyingly aware of their bodies the moment they wake up. Stiff necks, trick knees, tennis elbows . . . any goddess over the age of thirty has some physical complaints. Don't focus on them. It only promotes negativity. In any case, stretching will ease the kinks out of these minor aggravations. Five minutes— that's all it takes!

Do each movement slowly and keep breathing. You only have to do each movement once, but make the most out of each stretch.

- Turn yourself into a cat. Here's a wonderful opportunity to channel your feline influences. Elongate your body. Stretch it out to its fullest length and then quickly curl it back up. Now stretch out again and curl up again.

- Lift your arms over your head and flex your fingertips against the headboard. Point your toes and alternately flex and release the muscles in your calves and your ankles. Imagine you are a length of elastic and visualize yourself being stretched to your maximum length. Imitate this image with your own body. While you are doing this, breathe deeply in and out. Hold your pose in your maximum stretched-out state for a few seconds after you've inhaled. Release your body from the pose on your exhale.

- While still on your back, spread your arms out on either side of you, reaching for the widest points of the bed. This will be tricky if you have someone sleeping beside you. You might have to wait until they get up! In fact, these stretches should probably be done when you are alone in the bed. How can you steal these five precious minutes for yourself? Think of how generous you'll look if you offer your partner a crack at the shower first. You are being munificent, but you're also gaining a few moments to sensually indulge yourself. Sweet!

- While you are on your back in what I call the cross position (splayed out this way, you will look a bit like a ravishing, albeit crucified, deity), now open your legs as far as they will go, pointing your toes in the direction of the side edges of the bed. In this position, close your eyes for a moment and let your mind go blank. This is not the time to be fretting about the day ahead or the argument you had on the phone the night before with your mother. Banish such thoughts from your head. Think of a color you enjoy, something serene and peaceful. Maybe it's Aegean blue, or something warm and glowing, such as an orange setting sun or the pink of a summer dawn. After you have been doing this exercise for a few weeks, a color will instantly come to you the moment you summon it. It's only in this beginning phase that all this seems such a strain. Once the color is locked into your head behind your closed eyes, take a deep cleansing breath. Release.

- Still in the cross position, take one hand and slowly move it across your body. Begin by tilting your head back on the mattress or the pillow and placing your fingertips under your chin. Stroke the contours of your jawline and then trace your fingers down over your throat. Caress your own collarbones. You don't have to take a long time to do this. What you are doing is making simple contact, experiencing the smoothness of your flesh. The trick is to be mindful about what you are doing—hence the closed eyes and the blanket of color you've wrapped yourself in. Touch your breasts. Make note of their shape, their flaccidity or their fullness. Briefly touch your nipples. (But not if you're lactating. Touching them will only stir up your milk and you don't want to have to get up and nurse or pump just yet.) It's not necessary to tease them into a state of arousal, but if they are hard nubbins, alert, take note. If you really are not in a rush to leave the bed, you may use this time for an early morning self-pleasuring session.

Try This Method of Gently Pleasuring Yourself

Use your fingertips to continue your exploration of your body. After your breasts, allow your fingers to travel southward. Touch your belly. And don't get hung up at this point thinking about the diet you should go on or superficial crap like that. Save those thoughts for when you're headed for the gym or before you choose a bagel (300 calories) over a bowl of Grape Nuts (200 calories and all fiber) for breakfast. Touch your hipbones. Allow yourself to enjoy a moment of sheer personal glee if they rise above your belly like a pair of matched blades. Turn on your side and stroke your butt. Squeeze your cheeks gently. If you dare, run your fingertips over the brown rosebud of your ass. Next, run your hand down the side of your body from armpit to flanks. Turn over and do the same thing on your other side. If you were a cat, you would be doing this with your tongue, not only as a way of cleaning yourself, but also to connect with your sexual energy.

Turn on your back again. Now caress your pubic mound. This is your mons, your mound of Venus. Cup your genitals with the palm of your hand. Let your hand warm this center of your body. Breathe some slow, medium-deep breaths in and out. You may discover that you are growing a bit wet. Take that as a blessing. Not only is it evidence that your body is waking up, but that you have the understanding and awareness that it is Within Your Power—you, not somebody or something else—to wake it up.

Finally, arch your back for a moment and lift your hips from the bed. Hold this pose for a count of ten seconds. Come back down. Now you are ready to leave the bed. At this point, you may head for the shower or the kitchen and be ready to move on with your day. Personally, I like to follow up this awakening routine with ten fast push-ups and twenty deep knee bends, but you don't have to. Push-ups, by the way, increase your upper body strength. They are excellent for sex if you like being on top, tone the biceps and triceps, and strengthen and define the lats. Knee bends are excellent for firming and toning the butt and thighs and will give your body the strength to perform more strenuous and physically demanding female-superior positions you may want to execute sometime.

Why You Need to Whiff and Sniff

It's been said that our ability to smell is among our most powerful senses. For some goddesses, it is through our noses that we most experience the world. I don't have to channel back very far to recall the precious sensual scents of my youth, so intense and central to my core being and erotic center as to seem the very essence of me. Salt, sun, and sand are high at the top. That's no surprise, since I am not just a Scorpio—a water sign—but I grew up on the beach in Atlantic City, where in the summer, nearly naked bodies were placed before me to contemplate and admire. When you grow up at the beach, your sense of smell becomes highly eroticized whether you acknowledge that or not!

Smell, scent, aroma—the world experienced as you take it in through your nose affects your entire being. When we come upon a joyous scent, we want to immerse ourselves in it. Many of our most enduring impressions are in fact imprinted on us through our noses. Smell is also a terrific trigger of memory. Decades may have gone by since you last smelled a particular aroma, such as that thrillingly tangy aroma emanating from your mother's tube of Bain de Soleil, the greasy orange stuff that she so lovingly smoothed over your shoulders. Talk about an innocent although sensual experience! Many of our earliest budding erotic experiences can be closely associated with smell. It could be the chlorine scent of your middle school locker room where you first became aware of other budding female bodies. It could be the fragrance of the newly mown grass you lay on in your bikini as a teenager, proud if a bit embarrassed by your ripening nubile flesh. Even overpowering cloying scents can have intensely positive associations. Whenever I smell Brut cologne on a man, I want to lean into him, snort him up, because my first real boyfriend, Jimmy, always wore it. I associate Brut with his smoldering kisses and the intoxicating, hot groping experiences we shared in his father's Corvette.

School yourself to pay attention to the different scents and aromas all around you. Some, of course, will put you off. Avoid coming in contact with libido-depressing if not actually anxiety-producing smells that have negative sexual associations for you. For example, if a boozy-breathed man ever approached you, you'll probably never be aroused or have an orgasm with a man who drinks that same liquor. Associations with smell run both ways, good and bad. On a similar, although less distressing note, if a person with whom you are happily intimate begins wearing a cologne you can't abide, nicely ask them to stop wearing it and, if possible, gift them with something you both enjoy. Of course, not every cologne or perfume smells the same on each person, since the ingredients are affected by each person's body chemistry. You might have to experiment. Spend an afternoon visiting department stores with a lover—or future lover—to sample different colognes. Think of it as a kind of foreplay you can do in public with all your clothes on!

Wherever You Are, Start Sniffing

Another exercise to increase your sensual sniffing awareness level is so easy that you can do it anytime, anywhere. I find this exercise to be particularly useful when I'm standing in long boring lines, like at the Department of Motor Vehicles or in the supermarket. It is very sex goddess–like to practice sensuality exercises during life experiences that don't require one hundred percent of your atten-tion. Decipher which aromas sooth you, invigorate you, electrify you, speak to your inner core. Your eventual goal is to be able to identify which smells have what effect on you, and then to deliberately bring them into your home, your bedroom, onto your body if you wish, in candles on your night table, your personal universe. If you like, you can call this practice aromatherapy. The Greek goddesses did.

Here's the exercise: Wherever you are, start smelling. Really flare your nostrils and take in what you can take in. This is a lifelong exercise, learning to draw the outside world into your body and then to distill and diffuse it. Identify different smells for what they are. Sometimes smells can be very subtle, such as the pure, clean scent of fresh snow. Or smells can be appealing and obvious, like the heavy sweet aroma of a perfume like Tresor. Learn to identify smells that turn you on and turn you off.

Sniff Yourself

A more advanced exercise you can do to develop your sense of erotic smell is to sniff yourself. Start out by learning to enjoy the aroma emanating from your own armpits. I once had a lover who loved sniffing my underarms. At first I was upset, but later I got into it. Advanced goddesses enjoy their own genital aroma. Many women regularly smell themselves to gauge their own health. They know if they're unwell in any way simply by sniffing their own juices to determine any change in their body chemistries. If you've never tried this, here's how to do it. When you know you are moist, put your hand between your legs. Dip your fingers in your own private ocean. Now bring your fingers to your nose. Familiarize yourself with your most intimate scent. Don't be afraid of it. Do not be repelled. It is your special perfume, your individual aroma. Your most special partner or partners will connect and bond to you through it.

The Smell of Clean Sweat Is an Aphrodisiac

I can't emphasize enough the sensual aspects of sweat, even though the topic is an unpleasant one to many women. Most of us spend an extraordinary amount of time and energy, not to mention money, disguising or inhibiting our natural bodily aromas. I'm not even going to waste my time talking about feminine hygiene products meant to mask or floralize or otherwise compromise the integrity of the excretions of our vaginas. If there is a sour or very bad smell emanating from your vagina, consult with either a homeopathic naturalist or your gynecologist. The fluid that escapes from our pores, however, is another story. Clean sweat is, to many people, highly aphrodisiac. The physical sight of sweat seeping from your lover's body during an act of lovemaking may be enough to bring you to climax. Sweat is very, very sexy. Why else do you suppose in movies—and not just X-rated ones—they always show it?

Here's Some Good Things to Do with Sweat

Lick it.

Sniff it.

If it's on someone else, press your flesh against it.

Use it as a lubricant, like spit.

Wash yours off with someone who is equally sweaty. Goddesses call this "Shower Power."

Immerse Yourself in a Sensual Spectacle

This is a little kinky, although an intriguing concept. It's all about being imprinted by a visual stimulant. Shane had this story to tell:

Shane: *I was working as a magazine editor in New York City. For a few months, I had a brilliant assistant, a man a few years younger than me,* *just enough younger that I was constantly aware of the age difference. One day at work, he asked if I'd ever attended a live boxing match. He had tickets. That night, I accompanied him to Madison Square Garden, where we had ringside seats. He warned me that sitting so close to the combatants might have a few surprising consequences. The first match came on. After a few warmup rounds, it got quite aggressive. We were sprayed by sweat, then blood. The heat and intensity coming off the sparring combatants was incredible to me. It was like watching gladiators. The effect was both shocking and riveting. I could see their bodies giving and receiving physical blows. I could hear them grunting behind their mouth guards. I could smell their sweat and see fluids shooting from their bodies, flying beads of sweat pushing through the air. It was so primitive and animalistic that it completely stirred me. At first my feelings scared me, and I wanted to run away. Then I realized what I was experiencing was truly intense arousal. We left after the third match. Nothing happened between my assistant and me. That would not have been right. But the energy that was awakened from the sense of being a voyeur, from watching two men go at each other like male beasts in rut, lasted the entire trip home—even on hellish public transportation. Once inside my apartment door, I practically raced into the bedroom to unleash all that pent-up frenzy on my lover. It was some of the best sex I ever had!*

If Something Tastes Great, Put It in Your Mouth

A wonderful sensual exercise is to practice identifying different things with your mouth. A baby, even a tiny infant, first experiences the world by mouth. That's why they look so surprised when you introduce something new to their palates. That's why some babies look so pleased when they taste their first pureed apricots or pears or plums. Every taste is a new experience for them, something fresh.

Your palate is probably numb or jaded, and you don't even know it. If you're anything like me, and you must be if you are reading this book, you've scalded your tongue and the roof of your mouth so many times with hot coffee that sometimes you're not sure if you have any taste buds left. Trust me, you do. You just have to rediscover them.

You can get in touch with how things feel in your mouth and develop your sense of taste with this fun exercise. Enter the most exquisite gourmet grocery store you know of and make a beeline straight for the produce aisles. Forget those beckoning piles of zucchini for the moment: their time is yet to come. It's fruit you're going to concentrate on for the time being. Buy a ripe banana. The more mellow yellow, the better. Grab a handful of cherries, some raspberries. Pick a plum, a peach, a bunch of juicy red grapes. If the stuff isn't ripe enough, panic not. Just delay your tasteful sensual experience by a day or so until they ripen. You can hasten the process by placing them in a brown paper bag for a day or let them come to full awakening on your sunniest windowsill. The natural gases in the banana will make them ripen fast.

When the fruits are at their peak flavor, cut them up into bite-sized bits and toss yourself a fruit salad. But don't add any dressing—not your usual favorite raspberry vinaigrette or even a splash of lemon. What you want to focus on is the taste and texture of each individual fruit. Now close your eyes (a blindfold is better, but only with a sensual accomplice) and pick up one piece of fruit at a time and put it in your mouth. Without looking, identify what you are savoring. Don't immediately chew and swallow. Take your time to experience each texture. Allow the juices to flow over your tongue and across your palate. If you are sharing this experience with a partner, play around together by passing the fruit back and forth between your mouths. Should anything else randomly occur to you to further embellish the experience of savoring this delicate treat, for instance placing a piece of the fruit in your navel (or even more adventurously, your vagina) and bidding your lover to suck it out, go for it.

Seek Out Beauty

A goddess cannot help but be drawn to what is beautiful. What's beautiful might be an object, like a pair of chandelier earrings or a dramatic gemstone ring. Sunrises, sunsets, the desert at night are all enchanting, beautiful. Goddesses, particularly those who feel close to the special deities of beauty (Pandora, for example, was the first mortal to be turned into a goddess because of her beauty), find it difficult to tear their gazes away from another person they find beautiful, be they male or female. In acknowledging physical beauty, there are no gender boundaries. Very intuitive individuals can perceive the profound inner beauty in a kindred human spirit. If you are lucky enough to look at someone and see their inner beauty glowing and vibrating within, you are a blessed goddess.

Compiling Your Own Sexual Treasure Trove

Sexy Tip: Anybody you ever had a crush on or whoever got you hot is fair game for masturbatory inspiration. They don't even have to be real people . . . or available!

A woman never forgets her first lover or the details about what happened between them—intimate details like did he bite her lip, did he know how to eat her, did he or did he not have a big penis. A sex goddess doesn't just remember her first lover, she remembers all of them . . . and usually in extraordinary detail.

Enhancing your sexual nature and building up your repertoire of orgasms requires you to have recollections and remembrances—an inventory to return to on the occasions when the well of your masturbatory imagination temporarily runs dry. Even the sexiest of goddesses can use an occasional boost, something to get her going, some backlog of inspiration to draw on when she's in the mood to pleasure herself and there is no love or lust object present. That's when having an inventory of remembered acts, sensations, locations, and impressions of past sexcapades with former lovers comes in very handy. Your sexual treasure trove is a mental reference drawer you should be raiding on a regular basis. Trust me. It'll keep you tuned up.

An entirely different but equally important reason for having a sexual file full of memories about ex-lovers is that you can try things that you did with other people on your new lover or your longtime partner with whom you have fallen in a rut. (No goddess wants to admit she's experienced sexual ruts, but it happens to the best of us.) Men have an old saying that when you sleep with a woman, you're also in some way sleeping with all her previous partners. It's true. We do learn from former partners and all the different ways we made love or had sex with them. Just because a deeper or longer lasting relationship was not sustained doesn't mean you should throw the baby out with the bathwater.

The first step to creating a fantasy collection of your own is to review your sexual history and think about your previous lovers. The best way to do this is to put on your goddess cap and summon up their spirits. Some of you are probably wondering what I mean by "spirits." I'm not implying that these past partners are dead, only that, as lovers, they are dead to you. In reality, you're probably never going to have sex with any of them ever again. But while you were with them, you did have an energy exchange. At some point, you were on the same sexual frequency. That's the part you should remember.

It goes without saying that you should only be calling up the energies and remembrances of former lovers who put a smile on your face. There is nothing to be gained by recalling lovers who failed to please you or who only pleased themselves. You should be remembering specifically how one lover knew how to tease you into a near frenzy until you practically exploded. Or the lover who had a special finger action technique that always made you come quickly. Or the lover who took all day with you, exploring every intimate part of your body until you were limp and exhausted— TFO (Totally Fucked Out). Another point of this task (and what a pleasurable task it should be, compiling your treasure trove!) is to focus on not simply the sex acts themselves, or the size of your partner's member, but what sexual discoveries you made about yourself. For example, you might have learned that you have a more intense orgasm if your partner kisses your neck while you are making love, or that two fingers inside your vagina feels good, but three hurts. You may have learned that you come faster if you lightly pinch your own nipples while your partner goes down on you, or that you really don't like dirty talk at all. These are things that you discover about yourself over time, all of which is fodder for your own masturbatory imaginings.

My gorgeous goddess friend Roxanne loves amusing and pleasuring herself by summoning up the memory of Jim, a boyfriend she had a few years ago. Jim was a very inventive lover. Extremely experimental and into trying new things, Jim was the one who introduced Roxanne to the pleasures of oral sex. And she was desperate for it! Roxanne met Jim about a year after her fourteen-year marriage broke up. Near the end of their marriage, Roxanne and her husband's sex life had disintegrated into a routine bore. She described her marital sex situation as "the old in-and-out. Nothing more, nothing less. In and out. Three times a week for years." When she told me about Jim's boudoir charms, I instantly understood how Roxanne thought that, at least in bed, Jim walked on water.

The thing Roxanne most enjoys about recalling Jim is one oral sexcapade—a lazy summer afternoon they spent together when they made love four times. Each time was a little bit different. Jim kept introducing new elements. The first time they did it, they had a bottle of champagne. In between sips, Jim poured it over Roxanne's body. The champagne was chilled; Roxanne's body was hot. He poured a little at a time into the hollow of her navel and then licked it out. The second time, Roxanne took the female-superior position. The third time, they tried it doggy style. But the last time was the best for Roxanne. They had taken a break for a snack. Just leaving the bedroom was a novelty. In the kitchen while she was looking in the refrigerator for something cool for them to eat, Jim noticed a bowl of cut-up watermelon on one of the shelves. Using the kitchen table for leverage, he leaned Roxanne back on it and squeezed watermelon juice on her breasts. He repeated the gesture next on her belly and then her thighs. By the time he was lapping watermelon juice mixed with the nectar flowing between her legs, Roxanne was in a paroxysm of pleasure. She said it was the hottest orgasm she'd ever had. Now, whenever she sees cut-up watermelon, she gets wet because it always makes her think of Jim.

Borrow Someone Else's Experiences

My own sexual treasure trove is so large that I had to buy extra storage. Only kidding . . . not! I've asked some other goddesses to contribute their favorite memories. If your trove seems thin or bare, or you're just not old enough or experienced enough to have compiled enough satisfying entries, feel free to borrow these stories and make them your own. Explicit warning: The names have been changed, but nothing else.

Jamie: *During high school, I was on a summer vacation trip with my high school sorority sisters. While not many high schools have sororities, mine did—must be a South Jersey thing. Somehow, all us girls convinced all our mothers that somebody else's mom was playing chaperone, when in fact none was. Eleven of us girls crammed in three bedrooms, a bathroom, and a living room on the second floor of an Ocean City house. The floor was always sandy and the bathroom ever occupied, but we didn't care. We were spending entire days on the beach and walking the boards at night with some guys. Amazingly, we all met guys that summer. And we almost went all the way with them. I know I sure did.*

My third day on the beach, I met Will. He was tall and skinny and sun-kissed blond. His hair hung over one eye. He wore cut-offs. He was a few years older than me, a sophomore or junior in college. From the first minute he asked if he could put his towel down beside mine, I knew that before the vacation was over, we were going to get to know each other well—really well. Will was very good with his hands. I was a virgin, and my rules were that I had to keep on all my clothing. That was my only rule! After a couple of hours of sunning and swimming in the ocean, Will moved really close to me. Somebody threw a blanket over us, and that's what started everything rolling. There we were in public, but not, because the blanket covered us up. The beach wasn't very crowded anyway. After what seemed like hours of kissing to the point where I thought my lips might fall off, he slid his hand inside the bottom of my bathing suit. At first, his fingertips just grazed my hair. It was the first time this had happened to me, and it seemed so hot! Thinking back on it now, I must have been a very horny young girl, because I think I wriggled around before too long so that his finger would touch my pussy lips, which were extremely aroused and swollen. The ocean itself was a stimulant. All that salty water and being bashed around in the waves had excited me. After a long time of just teasing me ever so lightly with his fingertips, he slipped one finger a little bit inside me. Was I wet! My vagina was so slick, it was viscous. It probably was a little overwhelming, when I think about it, for that guy to have a young, truly inexperienced woman on his hands. Literally. It wasn't long before he found my clitoris. Up to that point, I didn't even know I had one. Because the fondling went on for hours, I had hour after hour of orgasm. Just as one would peak out, we'd take a short break—although I think for the most part our mouths stayed pretty connected—and then he'd wind me up all over again. It was amazing. It was incredible. I wish I'd known while it was happening that it would be the first and last time I would have such a multiorgasmic experience. It was totally mindblowing, but I took it for granted. I didn't know how good it was until it was all over.

Here's a good one from Shane about sex in a surprising location.

Shane: *The first time I saw Jess, he was beckoning me with a strawberry. I was walking along West Fourth Street in Greenwich Village, and this cute guy was waving at me from the back of a truck. When I got closer, I saw he had a big ripe red strawberry in his hand. When I was practically on top of him, he put it in his mouth with half of it sticking* out. I could have walked away. I could have just kept on going down the street. But I didn't. Instead, I went for the strawberry with my own mouth. The next thing I knew, I was kissing him. Jess and I had a very passionate relationship, even though it was brief. He was pretty wild— in truth, a bit too wild for me. He didn't have a car, just a produce delivery truck. He had a big old dog whom he walked on a length of rope instead of a real leash. He never did tell me exactly where he lived. Every minute with him was an adventure.

One night at eleven o'clock, he invited me to go around with him to all the restaurants he delivered produce to. He was collecting money, but we were having something to eat or a drink or Sambuca with coffee at each one. The last stop was a trendy restaurant on the Bowery. Third Avenue, actually. It was just a few blocks away from all the flophouses where the infamous Bowery drunks lived. It was a very dicey neighborhood and it was very late, probably two or three in the morning. We were both a little high. Jess had parked his truck near the mouth of an alley. He went into the alley to relieve himself. I was so scared to be alone on the sidewalk in that scary neighborhood that I followed him into the alley. After he finished peeing but hadn't yet zipped himself up, he pulled me close to him and grabbed my hand. He put it on his penis. The moment that I touched him, he grew hard as a rock. I don't remember now if it was his idea or mine, but I decided to pleasure him orally right there in the alley. I leaned against a brick wall and knelt between his spread legs. I grasped his penis, and he pumped himself in and out of my mouth while I played with myself with one hand. He came, I came, I swallowed. Jess let out a loud moan at the moment of his orgasm. Or maybe he shouted something. Anyway, a window opened above our heads, and one of those old drunks put his head out and started shouting at us. Jess's dog, who was in the truck, started barking. We ran for the truck and drove away fast. I had an amazing orgasm and it was a terrifically hot experience, but later I thought how awful it would have been if that guy had called the police. That's why I broke up with Jess. I knew something involving the police was bound to happen.

Now, when I need to, I just trot out this memory when I am going down on my husband of many years. It helps ignite me during what has become an otherwise routine act.

Sometimes when it's very hot in the room, it makes everything hotter.

Jolie: *Yan and I had been seeing each other for about six months. Just about enough time to really perfect our sex lives together, but not so long that we'd gotten tired of each other. There was more to the relationship than sex anyway, which was a first for me and pretty interesting. He was a foreign exchange student at my college, and everything about him, from his political leanings to what he liked to eat, was new and exciting to me. I didn't know if our relationship would continue at the end of the semester when he planned to go back to his country, and that added a degree of intensity to our couplings. We were spending the night in his dorm room, which was a single. It was very warm. The sun had been beating down all day and the cinder-block building retained all the heat. I had just taken my third shower of the day and was lying on his bed wearing just my bikini panties. Yan had set a table fan he'd purchased that afternoon on a chair at the foot of the bed. The fan was blowing right on me, but it was just blowing hot air. He was trying to study, but I complained that the lamp was making the room even warmer. He turned it off and crawled up next to me on the bed. He just had a single bed, and it was pretty cramped for the two of us. Normally I didn't mind, since I loved sleeping in his arms, but on a hot night it was just plain ridiculous. I was in an irritable mood, and the heat was only making it worse. Yan spit on his finger and put his wet fingertip on my nipple. When the fan breeze, or hot air breeze if there is such a thing, hit the saliva, it actually cooled me off. I told Yan to keep spitting on me, and he did. Every time the fan hit the spit, I got cooler, and then hotter, because he kept spitting on my erogenous zones. It was kind of funny, and we both started to laugh, but then we weren't laughing any-*

*more. We were making love. It kind of went on all night. After a while,
I didn't notice the room being super hot anymore.*

Savor the Great Moments

Now it's your turn to think about great sexual experiences from
your past. Go back in time and re-savor the great moments. At one
time or another, you must have made love in a bathtub or received
amazing oral attention from someone with an exceptionally gifted
tongue. Recall unusual locations, situations, extraordinary finger
techniques, the partner who could go on for hours, or the partner
who brought you to climax in one minute flat. You might have
to concentrate a bit to recapture these amazing moments, but it
will be worth it. The best part is that once you have developed a
catalog of exciting sexual experiences you have had (or even just
have heard about), you will never be at a loss for being able to
thrill yourself anytime, anywhere, at any moment when the
mood—or the moonlight—strikes you.

Fantastic Fantasy

Sexy Tip: Use your powers of imagination to the max.

---

*W*hat do we think about when we masturbate? What images pop into our head—sometimes surprisingly unbidden—when we are making love, our consorts upon us, toiling away to bring us to the highest peaks?

The woman who insists she has no fantasies is either a liar or lacking a pulse. Such a woman will never be a goddess. All sensual women have fantasies. They don't necessarily have to make sense. They certainly don't have to involve anybody you'd be involved with in your real life. You can fantasize about a movie star, the kid who delivered your pizza, your brother-in-law, your lawyer who handed you your divorce papers. Fantasies are an indulgence, not to be taken seriously. That's why they're fantasies. They're not real! Give yourself permission to fantasize freely, even about forbidden relationships. Don't censor yourself. Sometimes it's the forbidden thoughts that are the most titillating of all.

When You Fantasize, Shut Off Your Moral Censor

Someone recently asked me, "How exactly do you turn off your self-censor? How do you let your wildest thoughts run free?" It's an interesting question, and one not easily answered. There is no exact way, let alone an easy one, for turning off your natural impulse to inhibit untoward thoughts. It is so ingrained in most of us—by societal mores and values, religious principles, an accurate legal grip on the difference between right and wrong—to shy away from illicit thoughts, that most of us immediately blot sexual thoughts that don't fit into the mold of social approval out of our minds. There are some sexual fantasies you should inhibit. It's probably not a good idea to entertain fantasies involving incest or that involve physically hurting someone. On the other hand, if you think your very married accountant is hot, I can't see anything wrong with your fantasy of flirting or fooling around with him, as long as you don't actually act on your ideas.

Let Your Imagination Run Away with You

Whatever your fantasy is, once you get in the regular habit of letting your imagination run away with you, spend a portion of your day in what my goddess friend Joyce calls "free-floating sexual desire." The first thing you'll notice is how absolutely less boring your life has become. Fantasy is the enemy of boredom. And best of all, it is a font, a fountain, a source, a renewable resource you can tap into over and over and over again. Other women rely on their ability to fantasize to kickstart a masturbation experience.

Serena: *I like to think about past lovers when I masturbate. Or future ones.*

Samantha: *I usually think about someone I desire, usually someone I can't have. But if I'm masturbating with a vibrator, it's all over so quickly I don't have time to fantasize.*

Suzette: *I like to fantasize about someone whom I consider forbidden fruit.*

Some goddesses think of their fantasies in terms of a movie or a reel they can play in their heads. The "movie" can be very odd. You might not even be the star of it. The lovely thing about sexual thoughts is that we don't necessarily have control over them. They can enter, unbidden, into our heads. Some women are frightened or confused by their own thoughts. They may even have a sexual fantasy that upsets them. This can happen especially during sleep when the dream state leaves the door open to thoughts and images that the awake mind would immediately banish. When awake, the woman promptly begins censoring herself, editorializing, passing judgment, failing to recognize and allow for the fact that sexual fantasies by their very nature cannot be held to the same standards as actual sex. Is it wrong to fantasize about people or situations or even, as one goddess reported, members of other species? No! Fantasy is what happens inside your head. As long as it stays there, there is nothing wrong with it.

The best way to incorporate fantasy into your lifestyle is not to be afraid of it. Whether you construct a fantasy scenario (you're trapped in an elevator with your son's hot young tennis instructor, who in real life calls you "Ma'am,") or think about acts that would be illegal if they were anything except make-believe, the important thing to remember is that they are just stories or scenes you make up in your head. Fantasy only becomes problematic when it makes the leap into reality. Know the difference between what's real and what isn't, and don't fool yourself into thinking that it's a good idea to make your daydreams come true, because you can't. Helaine admits her sexual fantasies are sometimes way out there in terms of kinkiness, but she wisely doesn't worry about them, because she knows they are just fantasies.

Helaine: *I never think about what I'm doing. I have a random sexual movie in my head that changes all the time. I might masturbate to the imagined image of a bellhop I saw in a hotel lobby that I've never been in. Most of the fantasy situations I've come up with probably would not even be that enjoyable if they were really happening, but in sexual fantasy, they really turn me on. I've had fantasies involving all kinds of* *people and even animals—doing things I would never do in real life. The movies in my head are often rather deviant. I find this aspect of my imagination to be amazing, but it's been like this for me my whole life.*

Chelsea also doesn't try to censor her more outrageous thoughts.

Chelsea: *My sexual fantasy scenarios are always undergoing change. At times, they have been very romantic. I'm wearing something soft and flowing but sexy, and someone hot comes along and pushes my legs open and suddenly we're having sex, someplace outdoors, like maybe at a picnic. At other times, my fantasies are very forceful, like there are several men ravishing me all at the same time. Sometimes in a fantasy I'll be in charge of some situation where I am dominating my partner and telling him exactly what to do. I have a lot of fantasies about having sex outdoors where someone could potentially see me. I have six or seven scenarios going at any time that I can call on if I feel the urge to masturbate.*

Wake Up Your Imagination

Because we live in such a reality-based world, or because we're all so busy and overscheduled between work, our families, and all the errands and obligations that have to be honored or squeezed in, many women feel they have no time or energy left inside them to dream up sexual fictions. If you fear that your fantasy life has been asleep and undernourished for too long, Elizabeth had this advice to offer. It's so simple you'll be amazed you didn't think of it yourself.

Elizabeth: *I just pick someone hot and masturbate while thinking about him.*

Fantasies don't have to be elaborate. You don't have to feature yourself being fawned over by a Greek fishing god on a beautiful Mediterranean island, your body tanned and luscious, him feeding you grapes by hand one by one. Sometimes fantasies can be incredibly pedestrian, even stupid. It doesn't matter what they are, as long as you are experiencing pleasure in them.

Ann: *My fantasies are very boring. Really mundane, ordinary shit. Nothing unpleasant, however, just things I like to do. I've had fantasies that involve me going shopping.*

Other fantasies border on the extreme.

Giulianna: *I have a few tried-and-true fantasies that I rotate. They usually pop into my head on their own, which is a signal to me that it's time to masturbate. If I don't like one fantasy one day, I'll just go on to another. Sometimes a new one comes to me unbidden, and then I watch it in my head like a TV show before deciding to change the channel. One of my favorite fantasies involves going down on another woman from behind. Sometimes I imagine I'm wearing a harness and a dildo and I'm making her come. Another fantasy I have involves me being blindfolded and tied down while a man I don't know does different things to me. I love the restraint fantasy, because it means I can give up control and fully enjoy myself instead of worrying that I have to do something reciprocal in return. Other movies that I watch in my head are replays of actual sex encounters I've had. One in particular stars a lover who talked dirty to me all the time. Even when I'm masturbating, I can call up the memory of his voice urging me on, saying, "Come on, baby, come on, that's it," and whoops . . . it sends me right over the edge.*

Fantasizing about a bondage situation is not extraordinary. Closing your eyes and visualizing yourself in such a situation is harmless, and in fact might be a way to innocently let off steam without actually putting yourself in an awkward or even potentially dangerous situation. I hesitate to be the person to dictate when a sexual fantasy goes from being an erotic tool to becoming a real problem. The American Psychiatric Association characterizes fantasy as becoming a medical condition when the fantasizer begins to have obsessive thoughts relating to the fantasy and it becomes what the medical community defines as a "histrionic personality disorder, exhibiting a pervasive pattern of excessive emotionality and attention seeking." The histrionic individual experiences rapidly shifting and shallow expressions of emotion and often uses their physical appearance to draw undue attention to themselves. Their interaction with others is often characterized by excessive provocative behavior and the need to always be seductive. They often exaggerate the intimacy of relationships. The line between fantasy and reality in their dealings with other people becomes blurred. That said, should you be concerned about your own sexual fantasies? Only if you recognize that your thoughts are becoming obsessive or you feel compelled to act them out.

When You Should Not Fantasize

There are some women, however, who can't be bothered with fantasy. Reality is where it's at for them. A goddess might actively choose not to indulge in fantasy when she is with a partner she finds so inspiring, so thrilling, someone who knows her so well that it would be pointless to do anything except focus on pure sensation. There are times when reality seems more compelling than fantasy. Here's what Carole, Taryn, and Erica had to say about that.

Carole: *Fantasy? Not for me. I just concentrate on the job at hand.*

Taryn: *I never fantasize while I'm having sex or masturbating. I like to keep things real. Whatever I'm doing to myself or whatever is being done to me is what I concentrate on. For me, hot sex is all about staying in the moment.*

Erica: *I don't fantasize. I just enjoy.*

Fantasy As a Tool to Create Sparks

Fantasy is, however, a wonderful tool that can be used to create sparks with a partner with whom you are temporarily out of lust. It's easy enough to delve into your imagination and summon up another lover for whom you once felt passion. It doesn't have to be a real person or someone available to you. For example, you could be making mad love to your husband and fantasizing about the pool cleaning guy at the same time. Some women feel guilty about thinking about someone else while they are making love with their usual partner. They feel like they are "cheating" or somehow being unfaithful to the person they are with. Men, however, do this all the time. I personally don't think there is anything wrong with the practice. As long as your body is actually "with" your husband or your steady boyfriend, what difference does it make if your imagination takes you elsewhere? A word of caution, however. It's probably best to keep your unfaithful thoughts to yourself!

Sharing Your Fantasy with a Partner

Some lovers, on the other hand, are very receptive to their lover's fantasies. They may even enjoy hearing about them. Here's what Shane had to say about that.

Shane: *I have a recurring fantasy about making love with the guy who comes every week in the summer to clean our pool. He once saw me in my bathing suit, and I could tell from his expression that he thought I was pretty hot. My partner of several years was making love to me one night, and I was having trouble responding. I don't know what I was thinking about, but I know it wasn't him! Suddenly, the image of the pool guy jumped into my head and, just like that, I was wet and excited and ready to make love. I told my partner about it later, and he said, "Hey, whatever it takes, honey. Whatever it takes."*

Did I Hear the Word "Props"?

Accoutrements are useful tools to fantasy. Every goddess/actress worth her weight in gold knows the value of props. My personal fave right now is a velvet riding hat hanging on the bedpost. The simple sight of it fuels fantasies about horseback riding, riding bareback, taking a centaur as my lover. Wearing it when astride my partner, I can play the role of a proper English rider posting on my high-spirited mount. That is the beauty of fantasy. It can be about anything, anything at all.

To outfit your personal fantasy closet at home, consider that hats, stiletto heels, and boots are part of every goddess's wardrobe bag of tricks. Nothing gives an erotic charge to the boudoir atmosphere faster than theatrical adornments. On your wish list of sexual fantasy accoutrements, ask your personal Dionysius or your sexy Santa Claus for the following items: a corset, a pair of marabou-trimmed kitten heel slippers, a silk negligee, and a peignoir for those fantasy 1950s nights. Check out a decadent movie like "Far from Heaven" for professional styling tips. Or invest in a wig to see how you feel one night in your guise of raven-haired, sultry-eyed Maidenform minx. You'll need a push-up bra and a set of hose and garter belt to go with it. Channel up the sexy goddessness of pin-up girl Bette Paige. Ready, set, go! Goddesses, it's time to Go Shopping!

PART III

Loving Yourself

It is essential to learn how to give yourself the most pleasure so you don't rely on anyone else.

—Goddess motto

Masturbation and Self-Pleasuring Techniques

Sexy Tip: Enjoy your masturbatory sessions. Honor the time you spend pleasuring yourself.

---

*N*o one knows your body the way that you do. You are the mistress who holds the key to unleashing your ultimate pleasure. It is a kind of voodoo, a spell, a magic ceremonial practice we perform upon ourselves. Masturbation or self-pleasuring, whichever words you feel most comfortable calling it, is a form of meditation (and medication), an expression of self-worship. Paradoxically, self-pleasure is something we have been conditioned to be silent about. For many women, the admission that they masturbate is considered to be a source of shame. The very same ladies who guiltlessly indulge themselves for hours with manicures, pedicures, and facials will cringe and deny any intimation that they devote equal time to their bodies with their fingers or their vibrators. It's a sad state of affairs that our culture has developed and nurtured such unhealthy notions about solitary sex. Self-pleasuring has always had a bad rap because of the overriding Christian morality that says the only legitimate reason for sex is procreation. Wasting male seed as a result of ejaculate that didn't make it into a woman's body (the crime of the Biblical figure Onan, whose name became synonymous with masturbation) is named as a sin. In the Bible, a woman's orgasm is so beside the point it doesn't bear mention. For decades, enlightened pychotherapists have advised their non-orgasmic female clients that the solution to their problem can be found in masturbatory practice. Even so, legions of otherwise intelligent women deprive themselves of joy and pleasure simply because they can't overcome their deep seated and ingrained religious convictions prohibiting touching oneself or using sexual aids.

While some people (men, mostly) might scoff that a woman's fear or inability or reluctance to masturbate herself to orgasm is hardly a great human tragedy, giving yourself orgasmic pleasure should be a basic human right. Doesn't it qualify as the pursuit of happiness? I can't make a case for it more strongly or bluntly. If your goal is to enjoy better and more voluminous orgasms, get your fingers moving. Betty Dodson, a professional masturbation coach and author of the bible of female masturbation, *Self Love*, noted in a speech she gave to three hundred psychiatrists at a reception at the 2004 American Psychiatric Association convention at the Javits Center in New York City, "It's funny how we don't think of sex as being about skill. The sensation of orgasm is terrifying to many women because they are afraid of losing control." Dodson has fashioned an entire career advocating that women teach themselves through orgasm to practice letting go. The biggest problem she faces with her clients is to get women to stop holding their breath while they are pleasuring themselves or being pleasured. "Holding your breath," she said, "stops the pleasure."

No Right or Wrong Way to Do It

Where you masturbate and exactly how you choose to do it should be entirely up to you. The great thing about masturbation is that there is no right or wrong way to do it. Whatever feels good (and won't get you arrested for public indecency) is the right way. Many goddesses I have known have figured out methods of pleasuring themselves in public—ben wa balls, Pocket Rocket vibrators, clit ticklers designed to be worn in the underwear all day. One very enterprising goddess with whom I was acquainted always wore pleated trousers to work. Her secret was that every pair had a hole in the right-hand pocket. It was her custom to handle the brutal phone calls she received every day from her boss by standing up and pacing her office while running her index finger along her vaginal slit slowly and methodically and saying, "Uh-huh." Masturbating throughout these phone calls helped her keep relaxed in an otherwise agitating situation. The message of this story is that if you are a creative person and have learned the secrets of being discreet, you really can pleasure (and sedate) yourself just about anywhere.

Feeling Horny for No Particular Reason

Sometimes you might just feel horny for no particular reason. The word "horny," a slang term meaning to be sexually aroused, is a reference to having an erection or sporting a horn. The expression can be traced back to the 1800s, according to the *Slang and Euphemism* dictionary compiled by Richard A. Spears. Since women have no visible "horn" between their legs, until the latter part of the 20th century women rarely described themselves as being horny. Even now women are more apt to describe themselves as feeling "hot." It is in fact rare for women even to discuss among themselves what I would call random horniness, probably because to express such thoughts leaves them open to being thought of as sex-crazed sluts. As in so many areas of society, the old double standard prevails. Men are expected to walk around in generalized states of arousal. They are expected to openly have sexual appetites. After all, men are said to entertain some kind of sexual thought about every seven seconds. They are the ones who often wake up in a state of full erection, although most of those erections can be attributed to a full bladder, what some men refer to as a "piss hard-on." Many women are, at least at certain times, as horny as men. Because female horniness is considered unseemly or unladylike, women are less apt to talk about it. Here's what a few of the female correspondents had to say about their own horny moments and what they might do to relieve the itch.

Giulianna: *I masturbate when I'm horny or if I am with a partner and want to come during sex. I have found myself surprisingly horny while driving and have used my hand to bring myself off. I also sometimes get horny in the shower and use the handheld showerhead to bring myself to orgasm. I've masturbated while someone else is driving (with my own hand and a dildo), and I've brought myself to orgasm using the jet in the hot tub at the health spa. I've masturbated on a massage table (taking my time after the massage is over but before getting dressed). I've masturbated during phone sex using anything that is handy. I've masturbated watching porn. Let's face it: I'm a master masturbator.*

Erica quenches her desire to get off when she gets a moment to herself.

Erica: *I find myself sometimes masturbating in the mornings once everybody else has left the house. Then I masturbate either in bed or in the shower.*

Ann doesn't even have to leave her warm bed to pleasure herself when the horny mood strikes her.

Ann: *I enjoy pleasuring myself while I'm lying on my stomach in my bed.*

Carole took advantage of a road trip she took alone to satisfy her desire.

Carole: *I was driving by myself on a five-hour trip to take my son to a camp. The scenery on the way home was very boring, nothing to look at but trees. There were no other cars on the road, so I just began idly masturbating, mostly to give myself something to do. Is that strange?*

Masturbation to Climax As a Way to Calm Down

Sometimes the urge to self-pleasure just comes on randomly. Sometimes you might want to have an orgasm to help you fall asleep. Or you might use your orgasm as a way of comforting yourself when you're feeling lost or sad or lonely. I was a thumb-sucker as a child; now I might use masturbating myself to orgasm the way I used to suck my thumb as a child. It is a way of soothing yourself or calming yourself down. Just as I used that thumb-sucking to comfort myself, calm down, or put myself to sleep, I can use orgasm for the same purpose. Other times, the sensation of feeling randy or horny just seems to come out of nowhere. It's impossible to say what triggers these sensations, since it varies from woman to woman, and one woman can have different reasons at different times. It's just good to know that relief is relatively easy to achieve, as long as you've got a free hand and a private moment. That's what Chelsea does.

Chelsea: *I masturbate in my bedroom once a week. Usually it's just before I go to sleep. If I'm a bit sad or feeling lonely, I make myself feel better by masturbating. Other times, I might be stimulated into it by something I just read or because I was talking on the phone to my sweetie and it turned me on a little bit.*

When and Where?

The time of day (or night) you choose to give yourself pleasure is also entirely a personal (and flexible) decision. Sometimes the impulse to pleasure oneself comes in response to an outside stimulus. For example, it could be late morning and you're alone in the house. You might be in the midst of your spring cleaning when you spy something out your window that arouses both your curiosity and fantasy. Or you could be preparing yourself for an intense job interview and know you'd be a helluva lot more relaxed in front of your interviewer if only you could first release yourself from stress with a masturbatory session with the hand-held nozzle in your shower. Or you might discover an opening in your busy schedule when you have time on your hands and no pressing engagements. Any break in your routine at all that affords an opportunity to pay homage to yourself should be seized and utilized. Here's what four correspondents had to say on the subject.

Giulianna: *I love pleasuring myself in the afternoon.*

Kendra: *Any old time works for me if I'm in the mood.*

Taryn: *I like to masturbate whenever I've got the time and I'm relaxed.*

Helaine: *I masturbate whenever I'm home and alone. I don't use any power tools. It's just me and my hand.*

Masturbating When You Have a Human Sex Partner

Many women claim they have no need to masturbate when they have a sexual partner. I disagree. Lovers and the orgasms you share with them are one thing. Self-pleasure is another. Having a regular sex partner does not preclude or trump your own personal experiences. More important, it is my belief that you should masturbate even if only to improve the quality of your experience for when you are making love with a partner. Besides, most partners adore seeing a woman pleasure herself. It's a major world-class turn-on to be allowed access into another person's private erotic universe. Ann enjoys sharing her masturbation sessions with a partner.

Ann: *I'm less likely to pleasure myself if I'm in a relationship. If I can be with someone else, why would I masturbate? But sometimes I'll masturbate in front of my partner, mostly because I know it arouses him.*

Ways to Masturbate? The Possibilities Are Myriad

There are many ways to masturbate. Fingers are a basic way to start. Getting yourself off with your hand is quick, convenient, and very affordable. Vibrators are amazing, but they are noisy and can be cumbersome. More than a few goddesses, I reckon, have been exposed to the raised eyebrows of security inspectors examining their luggage going through airports. Even if you demur and say the device is meant for your stiff neck, not even the biggest rube on the security force is going to believe you. Another popular trick is to pleasure yourself with your bathtub faucet. The steady pressure of warm water on your clitoris can feel really good, but it can seriously run up your utility bill, especially if you're the kind of goddess who requires twenty minutes or more of a warm, fiercely pounding stream to bring herself off. Another potential handicap to this erotic pleasure is that you have to have a bathtub—not everyone does. Here is one suggestion from a real masturbation expert.

Serena: *I masturbate daily with my vibrator, although I do have another favorite way to bring myself to orgasm. I get in the bathtub. I have the water running from the faucet and I scoot myself underneath. It's very intense. It's also the first way I came. I discovered this pleasure as a young woman in my twenties when I first got my own place. I recommend that any woman who needs a release should try this method. At times I've come so hard it's practically knocked my eyeballs out of their sockets.*

Have No Clue How to Masturbate? Try Doing This:

The basic hand/finger technique is so easy, even a child can do it.

- First, cup your entire vulva with your hand. It you are right-handed, use your right hand. If you're left-handed, use your left.

- Allow your hand to warm the entire pubic area. This may take a few minutes if you are cold and it is wintertime. If you have not gone the route of the Brazilian bikini wax and still have pubic hair, now is the time to stroke it. Concentrate any hair stroking on the hair covering the labia (lips).

- Next, fully stroke your outside labia, play with them, tease them, roll the lips together, gently squeezing them, pressing them together, and then gently pry them apart. Imagine your vagina as a closed flower whose petals you are opening up. Lightly tap your fingers against the mouth of your vagina. Many goddesses enjoy having their partners do this. Goddesses who enjoy a bit of roughhouse sex often enjoy having their genitals lightly slapped! You might not be inclined to do this to yourself, but in the interest of furthering your erotic education, give it a try—at least once!

- Feeling a slight well of moisture growing? It means you are becoming excited. Now, using your second and fourth fingers, separate your lips. Use your middle finger to lightly touch your clitoris. It may still be hiding under its protective bonnet, or it could be erect and emerged. Don't rush into anything here. Your clitoris should not be the focus of your attention just yet.

- If you are getting wet, please continue. If not, bring your hand to your mouth and lick your fingertip. Then return your saliva-moistened finger to between your legs and stroke it across your clitoris. Experiment with different strokes. Up and down, side to side, up and down again. Some women prefer strong decisive strokes, while others prefer a touch so slight that it is almost a tickle.

- If you are a right-handed woman, begin stroking the right side of your clitoris. If you are left handed, concentrate your stroking on the left. Avoid touching the clitoris directly at this point. The area right beneath the clitoris is extraordinarily receptive to touch. Dip your fingers into it and enjoy the welling up of female juices. A primary goal is to increase what I call your "tease-it" level to cause mounting excitement.

- As your level of arousal grows, continue doing whatever feels best. If you feel an urge to cram your fingers into your vagina, go for it. If you prefer to keep stroking and massaging the area on one side or the other of your clitoris, keep on going with that.

- Don't make a plan for yourself or feel compelled to follow any kind of sexual map. There is no map. You're traveling off the road. Give yourself permission to fantasize about a love object, a past lover, a sexual situation you would thrill to be in. Or give yourself over to the joy of completely spacing out, focusing your energy only on pure physical sensation. This is your trip to bliss. No one can tell you where to go in your head or what actions your fingers will take.

- Go fast or go slow. If you find you're in need of additional lubricant, apply more of your own saliva or anoint yourself with a drop of K-Y Liquid. Avoid using petroleum jelly or perfumed hand cream. Both can cause an unpleasant skin reaction. Genital tissue is very similar to what is in your mouth. Anything you wouldn't put in one, don't put in the other.

- When you feel your body moving spasmodically or your leg muscles going rigid or any of the physical signs you have learned to recognize in yourself as a signal that orgasm is imminent, you have two choices.

- You can either slow down or actually stop in order to prolong the pleasure. To increase your potential for mind-blowing Goddessex, it's useful to learn to bring yourself right to the peak, to the very precipice of orgasm and then stop. In this way, you build up tension and increase the pressure; the end goal is to make the release, when it comes, even more powerful. If you've got the time, bring yourself to this About to Come stage as many times as you can before allowing yourself to have an orgasm.

When you finally come, your orgasm will be very primal and sweaty. You may find yourself dizzy and gasping for breath. An alternative is to bring yourself to orgasm over and over again. You can do this with your hand or using a vibrator. Goddesses who enjoy multiple orgasm masturbation sessions overwhelmingly prefer the power (not to mention unflagging endurance) of battery operated equipment. If you suffer from carpal tunnel syndrome, machinery is a must.

Varying Your Self-Pleasuring Routines

Sexy Tip: Try something new that you've never tried before. For example, learn to ride a horse. Practice posting.

*F*or many goddesses, no matter how much they enjoy and even luxuriate in their personal self-pleasuring rituals, inevitably for most women, even the most wonderful routines, repertoires, favored fantasies, and fantasy love objects become tired and won't get them off anymore. For many women, it's in their nature to desire a change in routine. These are not women who are wedded to specific schedules. They're not the ones who have been taking the same spin class on Saturday mornings for five years.

Many women have a craving for new sensual sensations. Those are the women who find it hard to settle down with one man, one woman, or even one vibrator. Or their needs change depending on their single or attached status. Roxanne and Erica had this to say.

Roxanne: *My self-pleasuring routines vary with my emotional needs. If I'm lonely, I tend to be very gentle with myself and might take a long time touching. If I just need to get off, I can be very, very efficient.*

Erica: *When I was younger, I rarely masturbated. But I think my sex life was a lot more active then. In addition, I was far less apprehensive about casual sex. Now I find myself masturbating on a regular basis,* *mostly because I don't have a regular partner and I'm not as comfortable anymore becoming sexually intimate with men I don't know all that well.*

Fresh Inspiration from an Erotic Movie

Watching an adult film certainly will give you new ideas. If you haven't been exposed to porn, you might be surprised. While eighty percent of commercial video sex is stuff you might never do in your real life and probably don't want to (anal, threesomes, gang bangs, double penetrations, monster dildos), nevertheless, it all provides marvelous fodder for the imagination. Just about every possible sex act and human combination can be seen on adult film: women with women, a woman with two men, a man with two women, entire shows dedicated to women making love with one another. Even if in real life you might never try any of these acts, watching the experience in a film can provide a powerful jump start to fuel new fantasy ideas. The politics surrounding women and porn are volatile. Anytime you put the words "woman" and "porn" together is a hot potato. As always, outspoken groups of radical feminists led by man-haters such as the writer Andrea Dworkin, who cried on the stand during the Meese Commission, decry porn as objectifying, dehumanizing, and destructive to women. It's not that they don't have a point. Undoubtedly, much of what passes as mainstream pornography is not terribly woman-friendly. But it's a big wide world of erotica out there. When it comes to pornographic material and sexual entertainment, truly there is something for everybody.

Tailored to Women's Needs

Certainly Candida Royalle's "Femme" line of erotic films are just that: erotic. Ms. Royalle describes her films as being "role modeling" and urges women and couples to study them to "model sexual behavior to use as a tool." It's not for me to say whether porn is "good" for women or not. Certainly I have watched plenty of videos that I found arousing and that incited me to send my fingers flying between my legs. Granted you might have to rent a lot of porn films until you find one that you like, but if you are curious to find something to pop in the VCR to give you new ideas to spruce up your sex life—including your solo sex life— don't ignore the opportunities that watching porn can afford. Chelsea keeps a stack of adult videos produced by Ms. Royalle in her bedroom to inspire her while she masturbates.

Chelsea: *I like to watch an erotic movie from time to time. It gives me new ideas.*

Acquiring a New Lover Can Change Your Masturbatory Routine

Many women find themselves more inclined to masturbate when they get involved with a new lover. Some women discover that if they've been celibate (without a human partner) for a long time, they may actually lose interest in masturbating, because their sex drive has gone into hibernation after going for a long time without human intercourse. Engaging in sexual activity with another person primes the pump, gets the juices flowing, sets the imagination into motion. A new partner spikes new interest in all things sexual, including self-love.

Meeting and making love with a new partner is a spur to new sensations that may also affect your usual self-pleasuring routine. I remember one goddess friend telling me that she had never had any inclination to masturbate with objects she could insert into her vagina. All her masturbation was clearly clitoris-based, or, more accurately, the area immediately to one side or another of the clitoris. (Right-handed women tend to massage the right side of the clitoris; left-handed women choose the left side.) But after her new partner found her G-spot, she got on the Internet and hunted down the newest thing in sex tools, a G-Spot Finder. Now that's her favorite thing, and she masturbates with it every day! Being with another person can reset your horny trigger and make you want to masturbate when you can't be together.

Samantha: *My masturbation routine has evolved or changed depending on how sexually active I am with a partner. If I'm not in a sexual relationship, I'm more likely to pleasure myself. If I am in a relationship, I masturbate when I can't be with my partner and am thinking about that person to the point of arousal.*

Ann: *I read or heard some time ago that men get hornier when they haven't had sex in a while, and women get hornier the more they're having sex. I believe it. I'm in a hot relationship now. Maybe that's why I feel more of an urge to masturbate.*

Hormonal Changes Can Make a Difference

Other changes that can affect your self-pleasuring routines can be hormonal. The hormonal changes that accompany pregnancy often provoke a woman to masturbate, even when she never felt the urge to masturbate before. Taryn found this out when she became pregnant with her first child.

Taryn: *I never masturbated until I got pregnant for the first time. I got so horny that I wanted to make love or masturbate all the time. Before I got pregnant, I didn't know what I was missing!*

When It Ain't Broke, Don't Fix It

What if you're perfectly happy with the same self-pleasuring activities and routines you've had for years? Some would say you are a very lucky woman. Lack of curiosity about trying something new is perfectly fine. If you're content with what you're doing to pleasure yourself, take this advice from legions of experienced goddesses: "If it ain't broke, don't fix it!" Here's what some of the goddesses have to say about their self-pleasuring routines:

Serena: *My routine hasn't changed in years. Decades, even. Why mess with a good thing?*

Jane: *I started doing what I'm doing as a child. I don't think I've changed my methods much since.*

Suzette: *I found a way to pleasure myself to orgasm a long time ago. Why mess with perfection? Besides, Vinnie Vibrator is always there when I need him. I can't say that about any man.*

Kendra: *I masturbated much more frequently in my randy, horny youth. I masturbate far less frequently now. Come to think of it, I miss it. Maybe I should get back to it? Just to get the juices flowing?*

A goddess-like Giulianna, who has a rich and varied self-pleasuring routine, has this to say about the subject:

Giulianna: *When I first started masturbating, I only focused on clitoral stimulation. Only after I lost my virginity did I experiment with vaginal and, later, anal penetration. I first masturbated on a bidet when I was 11. After my hymen was broken, I was hungry for things to insert and started experimenting with things like fingers and vegetables. I was in my early twenties before I got up the nerve to buy a dildo. Now I'm a dildo pro. I was a vibrator addict for many years; couldn't come without one. In the last few years, I've retrained myself to be more responsive to finger stimulation.*

Good Vibrations

*T*he vibrator, which is nothing more than a battery-powered version of the dildo, a distinguished sex toy that can trace its heritage back to ancient history, has been around for decades. Through the years, not much has changed in vibrator design. Vibrators come in many sizes, lengths, and widths. They are available in many colors, ranging from natural flesh tones to candidly unnatural ones, including those that glow in the dark. There are vibrators that have many speed settings, so you can experience a range of stimulation. There are vibrators that are intended for deep penetration, while others are principally clit stimulators meant to be worn—even all day long—in your underwear. Some vibrators are very small and meant to be used in the rectum. Others heat up; some even squirt! In fact, a person can become a bit dazed just contemplating which vibrator is the right one for them.

Taryn: *I never tried a vibrator. But that doesn't mean I don't want to.*

A Vibrator Primer

Suzette said she's never met the man who knows exactly how to pleasure her. She said, "Some things you just have to rely on yourself to get right. Obviously, I don't need a partner—not a living, breathing one, anyway."

American women's affection for their power tools is at an all-time high. The buzz on vibrators is that we love them more than ever. There are so many different kinds of vibrators that it's impossible to list them all. Many women like to start out with a simple battery-powered dildo that comes with a penis-shaped dong. Others swear by the Hitachi Magic Wand, the preferred vibrator of the women who contributed their thoughts to this book. The Hitachi Magic Wand features an impressive tennis ball–shaped head that can be inserted into the vagina. It's responsible for giving countless women who say they have difficulty achieving orgasm extremely satisfactory results. Doc Johnson, a major sex toy company, offers a very good vibrator called the Ribbed Realistic Hard Throb, which can be inserted inside the vagina or used to tease the clitoris and outer labia. A relatively new product, the Impulse Jack Rabbit, has been rumored to render live male partners obsolete. This vibrator has flickering clitoris-stimulating "rabbit ears," as well as a non-jamming beaded rotating shaft and a seven-speed motor with six levels of rotation. It's pretty intense!

If you're feeling reluctant to introduce foreign objects inside yourself, you can still have a lot of fun and plenty of juicy orgasms, too, with clit-ticklers. Joanie's Butterfly is probably the most well-known of these devices. It's a mini-massager/vibrator that can be worn right in your underwear to lightly tickle your labia and clitoris all day. The Little Jelly Tickler receives rave reviews from its users. It does just what it says it does: tickle! It's perfect for goddesses who adore those tiny tickling orgasms. If the idea of a big honker vibrator freaks you out, you might enjoy a vibe, which is a very slender battery-operated dildo with controls for varying levels of pulsation. Many of these vibes even glow in the dark.

The advantage to using a vibrator is that you can sustain an intensity that your hand can't always provide or free your hands to do other things to your body, like caress your own breasts. Women who are not entirely comfortable touching themselves often fall in love with vibrators. I will say that if you are reluctant to touch yourself, please try to get over it, or you will never really be a sex goddess. A vibrator can also be used with a partner, either to give him a break from thrusting action or for him to use on you while he is busy attending to some other portion of your anatomy. While some men object to their partner's use of vibrators, one very wise man offered the opinion that "Real men aren't afraid of machinery." Well said.

Here's what a few men who aren't afraid of machinery had to say.

Peter: *Sex toys are great. Sex should be fun. I'm not opposed to any kind of outside stimulus. I suppose I wouldn't like it if my partner got so attached to her toy that she didn't need me anymore, but I don't think that would happen.*

Mel: *I love it when my partner pulls out her toys to show me. I enjoy using them during sex as part of foreplay, sometimes even during intercourse. But I would be concerned if she'd rather use a vibrator instead of using me.*

Twan: *Women are not the only ones who get headaches or are sometimes "not in the mood." I'm secure enough in my sexuality to let my partner satisfy herself when she needs it. God only knows that I do the same for myself.*

Roxanne never used a vibrator until she had a partner who was comfortable about incorporating it into his sexual experiences.

Roxanne: *I never used a vibrator until I hooked up with a certain former lover. It was amazing. It was great. At first I was uncomfortable with it, but later I thought it was a lot of fun.*

Elizabeth favors vibrators because of the expediency, as well as the privacy issue.

Elizabeth: *What do I like about a vibrator? It's fast, it's easy, and it's private.*

The privacy issue is one of the main reasons most women buy their vibrators online. At the end of this book, there is a reference page to help you search for yours. Some of the most popular vibrators on the market today include the 9½" long Black Panther model, which offers sixteen functions and separate push-button controls. The world's most downloaded woman on the Internet, Dani Ashe, offers a G-spot discovery dildo that can be heated or cooled. Dr. Ruth Westheimer endorses the Eroscillator vibrator, which reproduces the natural movement that stimulates the clitoris by moving from side to side. The device offers 120 oscillations per second, promising strong clitoral orgasms that extend the vaginal orgasm. The Pussyman's Strap-On Party Kit comes with three different penis sizes for anal, G-spot, and vaginal stimulation.

For Suzette, a longtime vibrator aficionada, size and strength is what counts most in a personal power tool.

Suzette: *I use a vibrator whenever I'm in the mood. And don't give me one of those sissy things—I like big honkers with speed controls and big orange industrial-strength cords hanging out the window and plugged into the side of the house. Unfortunately, I don't use them as often as I used to. I must be lacking inspiration.*

"Big Honkers" Look Intimidating, but They Work Very Well

There are some big honker vibrators out there, and many women love them. I had a friend, S., who owned a huge one. I clearly remember being stunned the first time I saw it. I was visiting the loft where she lived and sculpted when I spied something that looked like a torpedo on her bed. When she saw my expression, all S. did was laugh. "Yes, that's my boyfriend," she told me. "And that's my husband," she joked, pointing to Jasper, her fat tabby cat.

One of the beauties of a vibrator is that you can use it when you're alone or with a partner, if you have a partner who is not intimidated by sharing you with a piece of machinery.

Giulianna: *Sometimes I use a big vibrator, usually once a month. The kind I use is electric, with a special clitoris stimulator. Usually I am alone when I use it, but I also use it when I have a partner and we're making love. I never can come from intercourse alone. I hold the vibrator myself—I've never met the person who can hold it right for me. I enjoy the regularity of the stimulation. It's a rhythm you can count on. But the buzzing is sometimes too strong for me, and it can make me numb or itchy.*

While many women do share their vibrator pleasures with a partner, the majority of those who use them say they prefer using them alone. Vibrators are reliable. They tackle a job and get it done.

Vibrators Are Not Only Efficient

Using a vibrator can often help you discover more about your own sexuality. For example, if you have been in the habit of pleasuring yourself only with your fingers, you may not be aware of just how often or how intensely you can come. With your fingers, you might experience one quick clitoral orgasm and be finished, whereas if you keep that vibrator humming against or inside you, you're much more likely to continue your self-pleasuring session to experience multiple orgasms. And once you learn what your body is capable of doing, you're more likely to keep pushing its limits.

Vibrators, of course, are not for everyone. But sometimes that's simply a matter of conditioning.

Ann: *I don't really like sex toys. I might be a bit of a prude.*

Can Using Machinery "Spoil" You?

Overcoming a reluctance to try a vibrator is a big step for many women. Married women are often the most fearful, probably because of unconscious feelings that they are somehow "cheating" on their partners by using machinery. This notion that machinery can undermine or compromise a relationship is one that has been reinforced by men who fear that their wives will discover them to be inadequate in comparison. Indeed, there are many women who find more orgasmic pleasure with their toys than they do with their husbands, although this situation does not spell automatic doom for the union. In a happy and mutually supportive sexual relationship, vibrators can be a blessing. And they can certainly add spice!

Many women use vibrators as a supplement to their sexual fantasies. Shane uses her vibrator to make her unrealistic fantasies come true. Or somewhat true. Or safely true.

Shane: *I have a fantasy of being with two men. One is in my vagina and the other in my mouth. My husband is stimulated by my fantasy. He enjoys having me describe it to him as I imagine it would be. Of course, I would never bring another man into my marriage bed except in fantasy. That's never going to happen. But when I perform fellatio on my husband and use a vibrator in my vagina, I get the double penis experience I'm craving . . . safely and harmlessly.*

Other women are wholeheartedly enthusiastic about their toys and how they use them.

Chelsea: *I love using a vibrator! I use one once a week on myself and occasionally with my partner. I have several of them, but I almost never use them inside me. I only use them on my clitoris. When I use it with my partner, sometimes he places his hands on top of mine so that he "gets" what I'm doing, and then I remove my hands and he controls the vibrator. Sometimes he masturbates while he watches me.*

Jill: *Sometimes in a lovemaking session, I like to go more than once. My husband and I are older. It takes much longer now for him to recover after his orgasm, or at least longer than I want to wait. So after we both have orgasms, he lies right beside me and uses the vibrator on me. It easily allows me to enjoy a second orgasm—sometimes even a third— plus he gets pleasure by being able to give more pleasure to me. I think of the vibrator as an extension of his hand, which I think otherwise would become tired.*

Samantha: *I use a vibrator a few times a month when I'm without a regular sex partner. And I have used one with a partner when he failed to "go the distance."*

The Downside of Vibrators

Trouble with vibrators usually begins and ends with how much stimulation you want and how much the toy can give. A longtime complaint is that they haven't yet invented the vibrator that doesn't make a racket or is subtle enough to please highly calibrated goddesses who only require the slightest touch. Those goddesses should possibly just avoid vibrators altogether. After all, they're not for everyone. Kendra is a woman who doesn't like them at all.

Kendra: *I tried using a vibrator, but I didn't like it. It was too intense. It rubbed me the wrong way. Maybe I bought the wrong one? Somebody told me about Candida Royalle's own brand of vibrator, the one* *with her name on it. Will a vibrator make you come? Absolutely. Does it make you sore? Absolutely.*

Chloe Wouldn't Dream of Living Without Hers

My goddess friend Chloe swears by her vibrator. She uses hers five days out of seven and yes, she has a lover, and a younger one at that! Ever since she hooked up with this man, her sex life has gone through the roof. Even though in her adult life Chloe has always been orgasmic (and this despite never masturbating in her adolescence, when she was a nymph), having a new partner opened her up. She says she is "hornier now than ever," and she is fifty years old! On the nights she is alone, she relies on her vibrator to ease her into sleep. "I use it when I'm alone. It's just too noisy for a partner to get into. I've got a big one and it sounds like a jet coming in for a landing. If you've got a powerful one, it sounds like that! I find I like the ones featuring a glass eye. Also, the older you are, I think more power is required. Another good thing about using a vibrator is that you're not distracted by a man. I make up my own fantasies and the contractions are much stronger than when I have a man inside me. Besides, I'm not big on pillow talk. I like to have my orgasms and go to sleep. I haven't met the woman yet who talks to her vibrator. Now that would be scary."

Chloe acknowledged she was sometimes made sore by her vibrator. "It gets very hot, and sometimes I have to turn it off. Sometimes it makes me hot and sore and I have to take a break and go in the bathroom and splash water down there."

Different Kinds of Vibrators and Where to Find Them

"Do they make a vibrator that squirts out a cooling liquid?" Yes, Chloe, they do. The range of vibrators in the marketplace and what they can do is inexhaustible. Anyone with access to the Internet will be amazed that by simply typing the word "vibrator" into a search engine (Google is very good), they can find sites hawking every kind of vibrator imaginable, including ones that glow in the dark, offer different levels of vibration and pulsation, or come equipped with silicone sleeves to cut down on heat transfer. These last are hygienically superior, because the sleeve can be slipped off for easy washing. Other models come with a hands-free mechanism. The newest twist are vibrators that can be preloaded with an artificial "ejaculate." Refills, naturally, are available from the manufacturer. If the idea of trolling through the Web for sex toys (and possibly crashing your computer) makes you anxious, try going to the Web site www.calexotics.com to peruse a wide range of vibrator models. If you happen to be in a big city that has an adult toy store, you can study what's available in person. The staff in these stores is usually eager to answer any questions, although don't count on any live demonstrations of the products.

More Thoughts on Vibrators

Carole said she had a vibrator when she was younger, but she never found it that enjoyable to use. She tucked it under the bed, and then one day when she was vacuuming she discovered it had rusted!

Other women who have dearly enjoyed their vibrators one day discover they have no need for them. They may have made a connection with a human partner whom they find more satisfying or rediscover the pleasures of their own hands. Other women who never thought they'd use a vibrator discover that the device can be a sanity saver to use between real relationships. One woman told me her vibrator has functioned as a lifesaver penis during a dry spell after she had become accustomed to regular intercourse with one partner, but then found herself at the end of the relationship. I think a vibrator can be especially useful to help one wean oneself away from a particular penis or style of lovemaking. A vibrator makes a terrific "transition man." Vibrators are also a panacea to the goddess whose consort has become unable for whatever reason to achieve or maintain his erection. While the two of them work to resolve their problem, either with counseling or a change in medication, truly the machinery becomes a vital "marital aid" in this context.

There is no shame in using a vibrator, or a dildo, or a G-spot finder, or one of the many other vaginal stimulators and clit-ticklers available on the market. Experimenting with a vibrator and seeing how far you can go with it will help you explore your own sexuality and heighten your sexual response. Most important, what you do with your vibrator—how you use it and what's in your head while you are using it—is a totally private experience, for you and you alone. You know how you're always hearing that you should make more "quality time" for yourself? Vibrators are one way to do it.

Serena: *I use my vibrator daily, at every opportunity, morning, noon, and night. I always use it when I am alone. I love the pleasure, the release, and my fantasies. They're safe . . . and private.*

How Long Will Your Vibrator Last?

It's impossible to say what is the "average" lifespan of a vibrator, although most of them do last for years. Plastic, silicone, and latex are durable materials. A key thing to remember about vibrators is that you have to keep batteries for them in stock. Imagine how annoying, not to mention frustrating, it would be to have the batteries die in the middle of a self-pleasuring/tension-relieving session! What happens if you tire of your usual piece of equipment even if it's still relatively new and in good working order? How often should you replace your mechanical partner, if you even want to replace it at all? Some correspondents share their personal views on what kind of equipment sex goddesses use and how often they upgrade it.

Giulianna: *Usually my toys last a few years. I'm from the "if it ain't broke, don't fix it" school of thought. But I recently switched all my latex toys to silicone, which is less porous and therefore safer because it doesn't absorb germs. I also add to my collection from time to time if I find a cool toy I want to try.*

Kendra: *I have one vibrator I bought in the late '70s. I don't use it very often, actually. I still have the box it came in. It's a pretty dusty box, but the thing still works when I need it to.*

Upgrading Your Equipment

Sometimes you find yourself using a vibrator you don't love. The reasons for this are myriad. It might be laziness or inertia or the idea of shopping for a vibrator embarrasses you. Maybe you aren't sure what device will work best for your individual needs, or that you're reluctant to plunk down money for something that might not work. It's true—you might have to go through a rather expensive process of trial and error to find the vibrator most suited to your needs.

Suzette: *Is there a bobble-headed vibrator out there? Partners never get it right on their own. I would rather get myself off. I never upgrade my equipment until the head of my vibrator has been ripped to shreds from so much use.*

Samantha: *I've had the same vibrator for about twenty years. It's a Prelude 3 Massager and it works like a dream. A few years ago, I pur-*

chased a vibrator that was in the shape of a large penis (battery oper-
ated). I don't like it as much, because the vibrating action isn't as strong
as my other toy, and the new one is a bit too large to be taken internally
for very long.

A Bizarre but True Tale

My goddess friend Guilianna had a gaggle of goddesses in stitches
one night as she relayed the incredible but true story about how she
ordered a vibrator online. "Personal massager, they called it," she
said. After an acute attack of sexual gluttony, it turned out her eyes
were much bigger than her vagina. When her discreetly wrapped
package arrived, upon opening it she quickly discovered there was
no way in the world she was going to get anything that big inside
her. She got on the phone to try to return it. "No returns," a repre-
sentative said. She tried exchanging it, but no dice there either. She
hadn't read the fine print on the order form strictly enforcing a "no
returns, no exchange" policy. She asked to speak to the customer
service manager, who, it turned out, was completely fed up with
dealing with women all day who were unhappy with their vibrators. In the end, she said she mounted hers on her night table and
draped a plastic lei of flowers over it. "It's quite a conversation
piece," she said, winking over her spinach salad.

PART IV

Adding Other People to Your Orgasmic Equation

Adopt swains.

—Goddess motto

All About Foreplay . . . or Everything a Girl Can Do While Keeping Her Panties On

---

Sexy Tip: Foreplay lasts longer when you leave your underpants on.

Some of the best sex I've ever had has occurred long before penetration. And I had plenty of orgasms, too. For starters, take kissing. It's a fact: that if you love the way a person kisses you, very likely you'll enjoy other intimacies that can be shared between you. But if you compare a long bout of passion to a six-course dinner, you can see there's absolutely no point in rushing head-long into the main part of the meal.

Kissing Step by Step

Kissing can start out slowly, experimentally. You can take a long time exploring each other's faces, first kissing his lips very lightly, then moving on to kiss his cheeks, his eyes, his nose, his neck, his ears, and then back to his mouth. If you're settling in for a solid kissing session, find a comfortable position that won't strain your neck. If your partner is very tall and you're not, try sitting on his lap for this first mouth embrace. Or if the lap seems too intimate because you don't know each other very well, have him sit on a desk or some kind of sturdy table. Stand between his legs as you begin your kiss. At first, don't introduce any tongue. But, you should be the first one to bring on the tongue; most women think a man who forces his tongue into her mouth too quickly is an aggressive jerk. While you are kissing, maintain a focus on the lips. Nibble the other person's lips. Try sucking his upper lip into your mouth. The best kissing is a "monkey see, monkey do" affair, where one person mirrors the other person's actions. Kiss with your mouth or kiss with your whole body. When things get very passionate, your entire torsos are likely to melt into each other's. Many goddesses report having experienced an orgasm this way.

Once your tongues are engaged in the action, things really start to heat up. A word of caution: not every lover appreciates the tongue kiss. Truly, it is not for everybody. Called a "French kiss" for reasons not clearly understood (it seems farfetched to believe that the French people, sexy as they are, were the first human beings to involve tongues in their mouth embraces), many very passionate goddesses do not like the sensation of another person's tongue in their mouths. Some say it makes them feel like they are choking or that it makes it hard to breathe. Personally I get really unhappy if I think my partner is trying to touch all my teeth with his tongue. What started out as sexy suddenly becomes more like a dental appointment. Don't think you are peculiar or sexually repressed if you find this contact unappealing. How you respond to someone's tongue in your mouth has little to do with how you'll respond to his penis moving inside you. Trust me on this!

Hands, believe it or not, are an integral part of any great kiss. Don't leave yours hanging by your sides. Caress your partner's face. Run your fingers through his hair. Stroke his back, his chest, toy with his nipples, all while you are locked in your kiss embrace. Depending on how much heat is being generated and how arousing the kiss, you can move your hands to other erogenous zones, perhaps by cupping his buttocks or stroking his genitals. Be forewarned. Most men respond rather quickly when a woman touches

their penis and not necessarily in the manner the woman antici-
pates. If you touch a man and he's hard, be prepared to move on
to the next stage of sex. Your touch, to him, is a green light saying
"Go for it!" But if he's not hard, he might be put off or embarrassed by the physical evidence that you're obviously hornier than
he is. This can be disastrous. Moving too quickly can break the
mood, fracture the moment. I've been in situations where actual
fights have broken out over a premature genital caress.

Petting

The next phase of foreplay (assuming you are ready to go to the
next stage) generally involves what I called as a teenager "feeling
up." Some people call it "petting." "Groping" is another good way
to describe it. Petting, feeling up, groping, whatever you choose to
call it, can be mutual—or not. I prefer to take a passive position.
I like to deliberately let my mind go blank and relax my body to
receive whatever tactile pleasure somebody wants to give. You may
not be able to do this with a new partner, just as you were fearful
of doing this as a nymph.

When you were a young girl, very likely during your early groping activities you felt it was your job to keep your defenses up. To
do anything less would get you labeled a slut. As a consequence,
even while you were enjoying a boy touching or kissing your
breasts, at the same time you couldn't fully relax and enjoy it
because you were clenching your thighs tightly together to keep
his hands from sliding between your legs. For most teenage groping couples, it's a struggle that can last all night. The point is, that
it's impossible to fully enjoy the sensation of your breast being
caressed when you're defending other territory. As an adult goddess, you may feel the same way when you become intimate with
a new person. His touch, smell, taste are all very exciting, but at
the same time you're unsure just how much of yourself you want
to share. Plus, you are unfamiliar with his touch. You're not certain

you're going to like it, which is the main reason you want to take it s-l-o-w.

Heavy Petting

Inevitably, although not necessarily in the same foreplay session, the next logical spot to be felt up is between your legs. This used to be called "heavy petting." Ideally, your partner will touch you the same way you touch yourself. I say ideally, because when you touch yourself, you know what's arousing and what kind of touches and how much or many of them and what pressure will give you an orgasm. It's a sad fact that some of the most otherwise fantastic partners are digitally impaired. They might be clumsy with their hands. Or the relationship is so new that you're still making adjustments to any new hands.

Comparisons to other partners are unavoidable. Your last lover had long, flexible fingers; this person does not. Or this partner has smooth, soft hands, but your last partner had sexy calluses and you thrilled to his rough touch. If you're experiencing difficulty in transitioning to a new partner, sometimes the best thing to do is close your eyes and give yourself permission to fall under the sway of a fresh experience. You very well might discover your new partner's unfamiliar hands are bringing you to new heights of delirium. Don't hesitate to give a new partner gentle directives on how you like to be touched. Show him either by pleasuring yourself in front of him or simply whispering your requests in his ear—two very effective ways to express your goddess desires.

Your Feet Are Also Erogenous Zones

Don't neglect the feet as potent erogenous zones. More and more goddesses are having pedicures, and not just because they want to look good in high-heeled sandals! Some savvy lovers have revived the ancient erotic art of toe-sucking. If you love having your feet tended to by your pedicure aesthetician, you'll go wild when your partner sucks your toes into his mouth. Many women say that having their big toe sucked gives them a direct buzz on their clitoris. Try it for yourself and find out!

Try Rubbing Up Against Each Other

Frottage, or dry humping, is an extremely pleasurable pastime. Like pre-intercourse teen sex, it's something many sex goddesses recall with embarrassed joy. To wring the most pleasure from frottage, you should definitely engage in it with some of your clothes on, particularly your panties. Getting entirely naked except for your underwear and having your partner press and rub his body against you can be an excruciatingly lovely experience. Your own underwear, whether it's cotton and absorbent (the better to sop up some of your love juice) or silky and slippery against your own superheated skin, creates its own friction, especially as the frottage continues and your panties are likely to get wedged between the outer lips of your vagina. In addition, the presence of a barrier to penetration works on the mind to increasingly heat things up. Just knowing there is a slim fold of fabric between you and your partner, that no matter how close your bodies become he is not getting in, is very exciting. You and your partner can enhance the frottage experience by grinding your pelvises together, rotating your hips, simulating the sex act in its entirety save full penetration. Don't be surprised if you achieve your most intense climaxes from a frottage session. Your male partner may not ejaculate, but you could, especially if during the frottage, his hipbone or hand is pressing against your G-spot.

Advanced Finger Action You Can Teach a Willing Partner

There are a few tricks you can teach your partner . . . him or her. It is my assumption, dare I say even hope, that some of the women reading this book are gay. Whoever your partner is (just, please, not a whatever—I love snuggling with pets lying on the bed, but that's as far as it goes!), what happens when he or she touches you between the legs can be a make-or-break moment.

As a goddess, it is within your realm to bestow favors. Telling your partner exactly how you wish to be touched is a gift. Hopefully, your partner wants to please you. He wants you to enjoy an orgasm. He wants to be able to gift you with his gift . . . the gift of his talented fingers, palms, thumbs, all of which can be used to stunning effect in the bedroom, or the shower, or any location you choose to make love.

From your own self-pleasuring sessions, you know something about how your body responds to being stroked and penetrated by fingers. When you bring another person into the equation, a few things change. Your partner can do things to you and for you that physically you're not as well adapted to do by yourself.

Here are some goddess tips and suggestions—proven, test-driven "finger action" techniques to bring on your own goddess orgasm.

- The goddess about to receive the gift of orgasm reclines on her back.
- Next, she raises her legs to a knees-up position and opens her legs slightly.
- Her partner reclines beside her.
- Kissing her mouth, he uses his fingers to stroke her Mound of Venus, or *mons veneris*. By all rights, he should stroke and tease this area for a long time, at least long enough for the goddess to let out a small whimper and further open her legs or otherwise signal that she is ready for more of his finger stroking.
- He should now dip his finger in between her labia to gauge the moisture level.
- If she is considerably moist, or even better, soaking wet, he should continue what he is doing for a little while longer.

- If she is not getting wet, this is the time to pull out the wetting agents. K-Y Liquid or an over the counter vaginal lubricant called Replens, both of which are sold in any drug store or supermarket chain, or even ordinary spit all work very well.

- The pleasure-giving partner now should insert his middle finger into his goddess's vagina. Ideally, his thumb should be right over the clitoris in the upper-left quadrant which has all the nerve endings. He should use his thumb to gently massage this area while his middle finger slowly searches along the walls of her vagina until it hits the sweet spot. Every woman's got one, although each one is in a slightly different place. She knows where hers is from masturbation. The guy will know he's got it when his partner lets out a distinct gasp or says "That's it" or "Stay right there." This is why communication is so essential.

- Orgasm, at this point, is imminent.

Want to Come Over and Over Again?

Steve and Vera Bodansky, sex gurus and authors of the book *Extended Massive Orgasm,* describe how a woman can have an hour— or longer—orgasm. According to the Bodanskys, the woman herself has very little to do with making the orgasm happen. In their view, the woman's body is an orgasmatronic machine (I made that word up) that only requires a skilled mechanic to get it up and running and running and running. The mechanic (partner, if you will) need only follow these precise directives: for simplicity's sake, I'm going to use the pronouns "he" and "she," but two goddesses can just as easily do this for each other.

The woman who will have the orgasm reclines on her back on a hard, flat, supportive surface. Her partner positions himself where he can touch her between her legs. She opens her legs really wide. Using his thumb, he pushes back the hood of her clitoris, while using his index finger to stroke it. He then slips his other hand beneath the woman's buttocks, resting his other thumb on her perineum, which is the brief flat road of skin connecting the vagina to the rectum. (The slang term for perineum is "taint," because it "t'ain't pussy and t'ain't ass.") He then starts rubbing the upper left quadrant of the clitoris, where there is a strong concentration of nerve endings. By varying the degree of pressure, the rubber can control the rubbee as though she is a marionette. Orgasm is nearly immediate; from the start, the person doing the rubbing can control and manipulate his partner to come right up to the crest of an orgasm and then bring her back down. These rolling waves of orgasmic pleasure can be prolonged for up to an hour, or until the one having the orgasms finally overdoses on pleasure. Here's the big question: When does one say "Stop"?

What do men get out of bringing a woman to orgasm over and over this way? An amazing feeling of control. Possibly, the pleasure of having his woman completely and literally "under his thumb." Another thing men get out of it is about ego. Giving a woman incredible orgasms is a major power trip. Imagine having the power, the awe it can inspire in other men, knowing you're the man who can make a woman come and come and come. Advanced skills in finger action are also an incredible confidence booster for any guy who might feel, even temporarily, inadequate or unhappy about his performance or his penis. To give his woman hours of endless pleasure, he doesn't need to take Viagra or respond to advertising promising him a bigger penis. All he needs is his fingers. Finally, it is a loving thing. What greater gift can a man give his woman than the gift of incredible Big O's?

Combining Fingers, Lips and Tongue

Finger action techniques can be used alone or in conjunction with other body parts, namely the lips and tongue. Some women find the combination to be too much stimulation and feel over-whelmed. Other women go crazy for it. Experiment with different things that can be done with fingers. If you've got a guy with big hands, teach him to make good use of them. At this point in my life, I know to look at a guy's hands. Any sex goddess worthy of the name knows that a guy's hands can be his most useful erotic equipment. A clever tongue and dextrous fingers are more enticing to me than a big penis.

More Tips from Adult Films

You can learn a lot of finger tricks from watching adult films. My cousin's husband calls them "training films," and on that point he's not wrong. In one movie, I watched as a man put his middle finger inside his partner's rectum while massaging her clitoris with the thumb of the same hand. He did have big hands, or at least long fingers. Guys who play piano, by the way, tend to have long fingers. There are other two-handed techniques that can be done by one partner using the fingers of both hands to separate his part-ner's labia like a curtain so he can lick and caress his partner's cli-toris with his tongue. The thumb and the second finger can be used to pinch together the flesh folds of the lips just above the clitoris, even squeezing it gently during penile or dildo intercourse. The little pad of fat at the top of the vaginal opening directly over the jut of the pubic bone is especially responsive to finger pressing or pinching. One woman told me that her husband gently bites her clitoris, and she enjoys that.

Teaching Your Partner to Pleasure You with His Tongue

*G*uys often snicker about other guys who know how to please a woman by massage. They may be snickering, but the fact is, they're jealous! A great massage artist is always expert at cunnilingus. Take my word for it. A guy who gives a great massage is a guy who is interested in pleasing you and who is "tuned in" to your body—who knows how to read your physical response to what he is doing to you with his hands.

You can save yourself a lot of time and eliminate prospective duds in bed by avoiding men who think massaging a woman is a big waste of time. These are the men who ask, "What's in it for me?" You should go out of your way to avoid men who actively reveal this kind of "Hey, what about me?" attitude. Beware. Most guys don't wear signs or have it tattooed across their foreheads broadcasting their selfishness. At first, these men may appear to have generous natures; often they're willing to spring for a wonderful dinner, although never forget, fancy restaurant meals are not just to impress you—remember, they're eating it too! For some men, if they have to go out of their way to pleasure a woman, they just won't do it. Some men develop this attitude because they're very rich or super attractive or have a big penis and no erectile dysfunction issues, giving them the impression that's all they really need to get by. They might be the type of guy who has grown used to having women fall at his feet. Or they just might be old-fashioned chauvinists. Whatever the reason, turn away from these men when they respond to your goddess aura and charms. Beware of any partner whom you suspect regards pleasure as being All About Them.

What If a Warm, Giving Guy Is Clumsy with His Hands?

Here's another scenario. You've hooked up with the greatest, most generous, most wonderful sex partner in the world. The problem is, that he doesn't have a clue what to do with his hands. In fact, when he takes his fingers walking, they trip! His distinctly untalented hands might stem from the fact that he's never had a professional massage himself and has no idea what you want. Or he could just be digitally or tactilely impaired. It's up to you to teach him, show him how you prefer to be touched, what feels good to you, and most important, how to master a few rudimentary massage (and later, cunnilingus) techniques.

Shane: *I knew this guy who was dying to have oral sex with me. All he talked about was wanting to do that. But I knew it'd be a big mistake to let him. He was so clumsy giving me a back rub that I couldn't imagine what kind of havoc he would wreak trying to eat me!*

Give Instructions in a Soothing, Calm Voice

Begin the lesson of how you want to be caressed and touched by leaning your chest against a wall with your back to your partner. It's very helpful if you remove your top and just leave on your bra. Instruct your partner to slide his thumbs into the hollows just under your shoulder blades and make small circular motions. It's better if he can use both his thumbs to massage under both shoulder blades at the same time, but if he's really slow to catch on, and can only manage one side at once, it's OK. Teaching your partner how you like to be rubbed can take some patience. Your partner may never have had a massage before and doesn't have his own body and response to massage to use as a reference point. Try to give your directions in a calm, soothing voice. Becoming irritated or annoyed by his clumsiness is counterproductive to your purposes. It's good exercise for you, anyway, to practice giving directions patiently and in a noncritical manner. By the time he puts his head between your legs, hopefully your patience will pay off for you—in a major way.

When your partner has mastered massaging the area just under your shoulder blades, verbally lead him where you want him to go next, which is probably your shoulders or the back of your neck. Tell him how you would like to be rubbed. Use action verbs to guide him. Use specific words like "stroke," "knead," "tickle." Mastering this language is essential for later, more advanced pleasure lessons, when you will be instructing him to "lick" and "suck."

Want to Be Eaten?

At this point, you could request a full body massage, but if getting your pussy licked is your goal, I wouldn't suggest you use up all your partner's energy getting your thighs or feet rubbed. You can either verbally suggest to your partner that he now direct his attention to between your legs, or give him the message via body language. Rubbing your crotch against his face sends a pretty strong message that few men can ignore. You can still have your panties on when you do this. Just tell your partner you want him to take them off.

How Do You Want to Be Eaten?

When it comes to cunnilingus (also known as "pussy eating," "muff diving," and "going down,") every goddess has her own ideas about how she wants to be eaten. Some women prefer that their partner's tongue never really comes in contact with their clitoris. They say the sensation is too acute, too extreme, and that it makes them too sensitive. Other women want their partner to suck on their clitoris or even nibble or gently bite it. It can get very confusing for the partner since every woman is different, and most women don't even want the same thing done to them every time. This is another reason why communication during sexual activity is so important. Here's what a few of the correspondents had to say about their preferences.

Serena: *I love direct stimulation of my clit during oral sex. It can be with a finger or a tongue. Even after my orgasm, I still want it stimulated more. After several orgasms, though, that's enough. It does become too sensitive. But after only one, please, please me . . . more!*

Giulianna: *I don't like my clitoris to be directly stimulated, even with a tongue. But over the clitoral hood, and with lots of rhythmic pressure, yes! And after I have my orgasm, forget about it, do not touch me there! I had a boyfriend who always tried to rub me after I'd come even though I told him, "don't you dare touch me." If he ever gets a chance to read this, I really meant it. I hated it when you did that!*

Helaine: *Lick my clitoris while you're eating me. But the moment I come, you touch it and I'll kill you!*

I can't overestimate the point of the overstimulated clitoris. Every female who masturbates knows exactly when her clit has had enough. It gets sore, it gets hot, the entire area, which might have been soaking wet with girl-juice only moments before, suddenly goes dry. When your clit hurts, the last thing it wants is more attention focused on it, but this can be difficult to communicate to a male partner. He simply can't relate, because he doesn't have a clitoris. The closest thing to parallel equipment is the most sensitive spot on the head of a guy's penis, but men who have been circumcised often can't relate to the over-stimulated clit feeling at all. When a lot of foreskin has been removed, more of the *glans penis* is exposed and the guy loses some of his sensation. Goddesses

who really think about men and their penile sensations often won't
have their infant sons circumcised.

Tell Your Partner What Feels Good

Back to the clitoris. Only you can say what feels good to you. It's
up to you to communicate that to your partner. Some women say
they enjoy their partner licking all around the clitoris, only grazing
it very occasionally. Some enjoy having their partner thrust his
tongue deeply into their vagina, imitating the movements of fingers or a penis. The only way to relay what you want to your partner is to keep up a constant stream of dialogue during the act.
Although you may be reluctant to be a motor mouth while someone is going down on you, think of the unhappiness, even misery
you will save yourself and your partner by having this communication. If you don't tell your partner what you like and he continues doing something that doesn't pleasure you, eventually you'll
discourage him from performing oral sex on you at all. He might
not even know why that's happened. On the other hand, if you tell
your partner what you like and don't like, and he counters by
telling you that all his other women have been perfectly happy
with his act, find a new partner. A man who believes that what
works on one woman works on them all is sexually deaf. He's
never going to be able to hear what you need to come or be a
responsive sex partner. Here's how Erica and Samantha handle
communicating their needs to a partner.

Erica: *I do like my clitoris to be stimulated during oral sex, but right
after I come, I prefer more internal action. I tell my partner to enter me
right after I come so that for my next one we can try to come together.*

Samantha: *I love direct stimulation of my clitoris during oral sex as
long as my partner isn't too rough or overzealous. Direct gentle stimulation works best! After an orgasm, I'm usually sensitive and also pretty*

tired, so I rarely want to be touched any further. I always tell my part-
ner this. But my recovery time is short—perhaps within thirty minutes—
and then I'm able to start all over again.

Some women love to have their labia be lightly chewed or sucked. Many enjoy having everything but their clitoris teased right up until they indicate they are about to have an orgasm, and when they say "yes!" they need their partner to quickly apply his tongue to their clitoris. Many women enjoy some finger penetration of their vagina while they are being licked and sucked. Others enjoy having their partner use a dildo or vibrator inside them while the partner works his tongue above the dildo/vibrator on the clitoris. In other words, there are as many ways to be pleasured with a tongue as there are goddesses who enjoy this highly erotic experience.

Overcoming Feelings of Vulnerability While Receiving Oral Sex

Cunnilingus is many women's favorite way to have an orgasm. Many women say it's the only way they are able to come when they're having sex with a partner. On the other hand, you might feel that cunnilingus is an intensely personal experience and until you know your partner well, you don't want to get that personal. For some reason, being on the receiving end of oral sex makes many women feel extremely vulnerable, far more so than when they're having straight intercourse. This might be because to totally receive oral sex, you have to hold still, relax, and give yourself fully to your partner. You can't divert attention away from yourself or deflect the other person by doing things to him. This is precisely why so many men love giving it. It's an incredible rush to have a woman under the spell of your tongue. For the woman, it's about relinquishing her power, albeit temporarily. But you can't really call yourself a goddess unless you're willing to sometimes let go.

Fellatio Has Totally Gone Mainstream

Throughout human history, a woman giving a man head was considered to be an inherently raunchy act. The Kama Sutra, the great Eastern Indian guide to sexual pleasure, actually cautions men against engaging in it unless the one on his or her knees doing the sucking is either a eunuch (a castrated man) or a female prostitute. Sucking a man's penis in the Kama Sutra is considered far too animalistic an activity for an honored wife or cherished lover. Fellatio falls into a category of sex the Eastern Indians call "low congress," so called because "low" means animalistic. But the sweet 'n' low-down, as I call it, can be very exciting, and that is why I urge all sex goddesses to try it.

You do not have to be an expert fellatrix to call yourself a goddess. Plenty of women never, ever, give head, and yet their husbands worship and adore them. Contrary to popular belief, not all men "live for head," and many secretly think fellatio is such a dirty act that they are appalled when their "nice" partners suggest it. This is particularly true of older men, who like to put their goddesses up on pedestals. The problem with pedestals is that when you've been put up on a perch, you can miss out on the hot action going on at ground level—the sweet 'n' low-down. I don't think you have to give your partner head every time. In fact, I resent the idea that all foreplay must include fellatio—how unimaginative! Sometimes a woman should give her man head just for head's sake . . . his head and her own.

Coming Whilst Giving

I asked two of my most sensuous goddess friends if they had experienced an orgasm while giving a male partner head. I wondered what, beyond proving their skills (and, oh yes, pleasuring their partners), they got out of it. Here's what they said.

Lucia: *I have had an orgasm while giving my partner the gift of fellatio, but not regularly. There definitely is a big turn-on factor to the act, especially (and perhaps only) when accompanied by mutually deep feelings for the other, which is the only time I believe sex is really good, anyway . . . and, I would advise my children, the only time one should have sex. The act is sexually stimulating in many ways. It probably is at least half inexplicable, pure, primitive instinct. Then there's the excitement of pleasing your partner, plus how he responds to you . . . with that interplay and expressiveness of both partners feeding the excitement and heightening the experience. Fellatio can stimulate all the senses and, clinically speaking, promotes feminine lubrication. It builds desire.*

Vanessa: *I know it's possible to have an orgasm without stimulation, or there wouldn't be such things as "wet dreams." (I've had those a few times.) But I have never climaxed while awake and giving a guy head without touching myself or being touched. But I do get turned on, i.e., very wet, when I'm doing it. Some of the factors of my excitement: 1) the guy's reactions (moans, movements, words, the fact that I have the power to make him lose control), 2) the images from porn movies that inevitably show up in my head (which I've learned from, and which prompt me to exercise my expertise in fellatio!), and 3) knowing I'll get mine in return! Sometimes I masturbate while I'm doing it, but not usually to orgasm. Of course, if one is lucky, one can be penetrated or get licked to orgasm at the same time one is giving head.*

Tips and Tricks for Giving the Best Head

Here are some of my favorite goddess tips and tricks about giving head:

- Make sure your mouth is plenty wet. You can't have too much saliva to do the job right.
- If you've got prominent front teeth, practice covering them

with your lips and tongue. No guy likes to get nicked or bitten.

- At first, just concentrate on the head of the penis. Take your time working your way down the shaft.

- Don't play with or bounce or suck or lick a guy's balls unless you've found out first if this is something he enjoys. It's up to you how you're going to extract that information. It might seem awkward to ask a guy just how much (or little) he enjoys having his balls played with, but sometimes it's less awkward to just open your mouth and ask, rather than do it and have him yell "Ouch!"

- The secret to deep-throating (taking most or all of the shaft into your mouth/throat) is to overcome the gag reflex. This can be done by practice. The trick is to keep swallowing while you are sucking. It keeps air and saliva flowing and is the only way to override your body's natural urge to gag because something is blocking your throat.

- Vary your movements. Lick the guy's penis as though it were a lollipop. Then twirl your tongue all around it like it's a dripping ice cream cone. Suck on it for a while and then return to licking. If your partner requires a piston-like movement, please try to work it out. This can be a tough test of your neck muscles, your breathing skills, and your ability to keep making more spit.

- Don't ignore the male perineum, the little road of flesh between the balls and the rectum. Lick it. Sniff it. You may discover you love the male smell that can be inhaled so succinctly there. This may be an acquired smell preference.

- Should you absolutely, positively feel obliged to swallow? Most guys love it when a woman will take them the whole road to China and allow them to come in their mouths. If you can do it, that's wonderful. Your partner will be ecstatic.

But if you can't bring yourself to it because it makes you gag or you intensely dislike the taste of semen (remember, no asparagus for dinner if fellatio is on the dessert menu), encourage your partner to ejaculate on your breasts or, if you can handle it, on your face. A lot of men go crazy for the latter. In fact, in porn films it's even a specific act. It's called . . . what else? . . . a "facial."

Pick a Position

*K*nees up, knees down, doggy style, missionary—what most women in search of the ultimate orgasm want to know is what position will make them come? The answer is that there is no right answer. If only it were that simple!

Even though the Kama Sutra lists dozens of positions for having sex, most women find themselves in one of three positions: that is Missionary (woman on her back beneath the man), Rear Entry (man entering the woman from behind, usually while both of them are on their knees), and Female Superior (woman on top). Variations of these postures include Reverse Cowgirl (woman on top but facing away from the man), various leg postures that the woman can assume while she is on her back beneath the man, and rear approaches done while both parties are standing up, the woman usually braced for balance against a solid surface, such as a wall.

Female Superior Position

The female superior position is the one most cited by women as being conducive to the feminine orgasm. Many women insist it is the only guaranteed way for them to come. The female superior position has a lot going for it. The woman can control the action. She can control the speed, the depth, the angle. She can adjust the angle to her own liking throughout the love bout simply by shift-

is generously proportioned and her partner enjoys the
of being somewhat dominated by a larger female. The
also may be exhilarated by their uneven proportions and
ation of dominance. Sometimes that dominance is the key
getting off.

*I like to be on top. I don't think it's a control issue (as some men
accused me!), but more of a weight issue.*

Rear Entry, Otherwise Known as "Doggy Style"

gy-style, or rear entry of the vagina (not to be confused with
sex, which is penetration of the rectum), is a very satisfying
ition to achieve deep penetration, although some women with
orter, shallower vaginas say they find the position uncomfort-
le. Rear entry is achieved by the woman facing away from her
artner and either bending over a table or the hood of a car
something stable is necessary to balance her body) or on a bed
on her knees with her upper body supported by her elbows. In
the rear entry position, the partners are prohibited from really
seeing each other's faces. This can be wonderful if you are deep
into your own full-blown sexual fantasy that does not necessarily
include the person who is penetrating you. On the other hand, if
what you're striving for is an intimate, face-to-face connection
where you and your partner can easily communicate, this may not
be your favorite position. Many women love it, however, because
of the potential for deeper vaginal penetration. Serena, Carole, and
Guilianna have this to say about it.

Serena: *The doggy style is the most intense to me, although it doesn't
guarantee orgasm.*

Giulianna: *I like doggy style masturbation, which always works for me.
I get on the bed, put myself in a kneeling position, put my head on the*

ing her body or changing the position
female superior position, she can crou
using her thighs for leverage, or she can
him. This position also promotes nor
between the partners, as it allows the woma
ner's face and to be able to kiss, caress, nuzz
bite (make that nibble, unless you're into the
neck, shoulders, upper arms, and torso.

My goddess friend Jane's particular version
rior position calls for mounting her partner's bo
the bed. She prefers to keep her knees on either s
planted on the mattress, and then angle her uppe
she were a bird in flight. She likes her breasts to da
ner's face, the better for him to kiss and lick them.
feeling of being in control of the action, with her doir
work while her partner remains relatively passive. She
she really requires of the man is that he have a solid e

The female superior position as outlined above
devoted fans.

Samantha: *It has to be me on top, definitely. But I have to
tioned in a certain way so that I get both the internal and extern
ulation. The posture is generally one of starting off almost squattin
my partner, and then, when I feel close to climax, I extend my leg
wide straddle over my partner. There seems to be more direct fri
between the clitoris and the shaft of the penis in this position, as wel
the sensation of vaginal penetration.*

Being on top is an excellent choice of position if the partners'
heights and weights are mismatched. A petite woman usually
prefers to be on top of a much larger man. Being on top means
she won't get pinned beneath him, and they'll both have more
flexibility for her to move around. But the reverse can be true if the

goddess
feeling
woman
her sens
to her

Erica:
have

Dog
ana
pos
sh
ab
p
(

pillow, reach around behind and get to work using my hand or my vibrator. Works like a shot every time.

Carole: *Doggy style is my favorite position. What I like is that a man can penetrate me more deeply from this position. I like the man behind me on his knees, with me on my knees.*

The Missionary Position

Although it is often ridiculed and much maligned, the so-called missionary position is truly the most popular and certainly the most classic. The missionary position is wonderful for women because they can Just Lie Back and Relax. Many women prefer the missionary position either because it puts very little demand on them in the way of movement, or because they are totally comfortable with the idea of just allowing themselves to be pleasured. In the missionary position, a woman can literally do nothing, if that is what she wants to do. Her job, in this position, is simply to receive. In the missionary position, the man is free to set the pace, control the depth of the penetration, massage, caress, finger, and lick other parts of his partner's body with his hands, lips, and tongue. The two can maintain eye contact and easily verbally communicate during the sex act. The woman can add variety by lifting her hips, raising her knees, planting her feet against her partner's chest, or draping them over his shoulders, if she is flexible enough and if she pleases. Some women like to embrace the man around his waist with their legs, squeezing him tightly at the moment of her orgasm. The missionary position allows for a full spectrum of variations and can be easily used in conjunction with other positions. Many women who enjoy longer bouts of sex prefer having their partner end the love session in the missionary position after they've explored other positions as an extended form of foreplay. Winding up a protracted act of passionate physical love in the missionary position can be exceptionally sweet.

Elizabeth: *Missionary is my favorite position, I must admit.*

Roxanne: *I love the missionary position. I keep my knees up, way up, and that usually guarantees an orgasm for me.*

Here's what some men have to say about pleasing their goddesses and what positions they've found pleasure them.

Peter: *There are certain things I'll do to give a woman an orgasm because I've seen them work, they're effective, and they turn me on. But I usually rely on the woman to let me know if there is something that is particularly erotic to her. She should talk to me while we're making love, or at least sigh, purr, or give some indication that what I'm doing is pleasing her. I definitely want to do anything and everything I can to please her, and the "dirtier" it is, the more I like it.*

Mel knows that no two women respond the same way.

Mel: *I have found tricks that vary from partner to partner, but I've learned that no two women respond the same. The trick is to discover what that trick is to each lover. That's part of the fun—finding out what she likes. Sometimes it's a matter of trial and error, but the road to pleasure is just another journey you have to be willing to travel on. My current relationship is new, so I haven't discovered all the tricks that can be found yet, but one technique I have discovered that seems to work well with her is that I massage her clitoris with my index finger while massaging the inside of her vaginal lips with my other three fingers. She also has a sexual position that seems to work for her most of the time, which is female superior (woman on top).*

Alec doesn't like to mess around when he wants his partner to come. Positions take a backseat in his opinion. In his experience, it's all about the tongue.

Alec: *No position is "the position," in my opinion. Whatever position she is in, I've found using my tongue on a woman is the best way to guarantee her an orgasm. After she's come, she's usually open to any position I feel like putting her in.*

Here's what Ray, a very wise man, had to say.

Ray: *I don't think the position is really that important, although some women are very hung up on specific ones or have ones they won't try. To me, it's less about position than working to stay in tune with her needs and her desires. That's where I choose to devote my full attention.*

Keith has an entirely different perspective.

Keith: *Position? The woman will do all the work if you do 'em right.*

For Curt, it's less about positions than it is about process.

Curt: *Focusing on positions or even on orgasms is the least pleasurable way to be during lovemaking, I think. Focusing on the particulars, like what kind of pretzel positions you can get in or what kind of orgasm any special position is supposed to have, is wrong to me. Position-oriented orgasm is all about performance and goal orientation and is, in my humble opinion, counterproductive to deep and meaningful sex.*

Be an Animal: Tickling, Wrestling, Love Bites, and Aggressive Love Play

*W*hen you delve into the mythology of goddessness, you'll quickly discover that these gals were anything but wimps. Queen Medb, a pre-Christian goddess of the Celts and focus of many Celtic myths, was a wild woman. Known as the warrior queen of Connacht, she held unwavering power over men, both with her courage and her sexual allure. Her libido rivaled her male counterparts, and she had many lovers despite being married to her husband, Ailill. Medb is a wonderful example of a powerful feminine entity, a formidable woman unafraid of exhibiting her animal nature.

Humans entered this world as quadrupeds; no matter what finery you clothe yourself in, no matter which car you drive, whether or not you wax or shave off your body hair, you are still an animal, a mammal, a warm-blooded, passionate creature. There will be times when you want to be the sexual aggressor. Most men love this. It's erotically thrilling to see a partner occasionally transformed into a tigress.

Here's Mack's point of view.

Mack: *When a woman is acting as the aggressor and she's just a bit rough, it adds another emotion to the erotic mix. There's a level of fear and a level of trust when teeth are involved. It's very thrilling. You're not one hundred percent sure what's going to happen next. You love what* *she's doing, but there's a tiny element of danger. Is she going to actually bite your penis . . . or not?*

The Instinct to Claim Our Lovers

Like the tigers, leopards, bears, and even mice who mark their mates (mostly with urine and secretions from their glands), we have an instinct to claim our lovers, somehow mark them as our own. You could say it's a deep-seated, hard-wired, territorial thing. During very hot passionate sex, lovers can get carried away. They become more animalistic. They squeeze. They clutch. Sometimes they bite and scratch. Hot lovemaking can leave bruises. The Kama Sutra discusses this urge to mark our lovers in detail, going so far as to offer explicit, guided directives on just how many marks one can leave, what kinds of marks they are, and what portions of the body can be marked. In the section on sexual union, Part Four is entitled "On Pressing or Marking with the Nails." Acceptable locations to scratch your partner's flesh are the armpits, the throat, the breasts, lips, belly, and thighs. Five marks of the nails made near the nipple is called, "the jump of the hare." Today, our society and culture and the particular period of human history in which we live has bleached out this very animalistic aspect of carnal behavior.

I am not an advocate of leaving bite and scratch marks on lovers, although I recognize the appeal. There is a strong urge among goddesses to stake our claim on our partners. If giving your lover a hickey or leaving a ring of tiny bite marks around his nipples turns you both on, go for it. And the marking can go the other way. You might have a lover who can't resist occasionally leaving a tooth mark or two on you. Territoriality often runs in two directions. But beware of the lover who repeatedly marks you. I hate to say it, but very passionate unions involving rough sex have a tendency to wind up in family court.

The Kama Sutra Compares Sex to a Quarrel

Splendid if cumbersome directives on the art of violent lovemaking can be found in the Kama Sutra, the great Indian bible of love. Sexual intercourse, it says, can be compared to a quarrel, on account of the contrary nature of love and the tendency to dispute. In its section on the "various modes of striking and the sounds appropriate to them," the Kama Sutra mentions that "blows with the fist should be given on the back of the woman while she is sitting on the lap of the man, and that she should give blows in return, abusing the man as if she were angry, while making the cooing and weeping sounds of a dove." Unfortunately for modern readers, the text is too awkward and cumbersome or even frightening for most people—even goddesses—to read. Translated from the Sanskrit in 1883 by Sir Richard Burton and F. F. Arbuthnot, legendary adventurers who brought to an English speaking audience the ancient text of Vatsayana, a writer who lived between the first and fourth centuries A.D., the language of the book today seems impossibly stuffy, even ridiculous. Not too many Western readers can appreciate that "the women of Avantika are fond of foul pleasures and have not good manners." I will share here what I've extracted from the portions of the text devoted to the art of tickling, wrestling, squeezing, scratching, and love bites. Suck this information up like a sponge. Knowledge of these very special arts is part of your sexual arsenal.

Bruising Kisses

Deep kissing—what I call the bruising kind—is the first step toward orgasm. Unless you're pleasuring yourself, when you're with a partner it's easier to come when you've been kissing. A magical mystery cord of nerves and transmitters connects the mouth to the vulva. When one mouth is aroused, so is the other.

It doesn't matter who begins the deep kissing. The kiss can flow into a soft nibble. It might stay at that level, the lovers sucking and chewing on each other's lips like they are candy. This kind of lip-chewing kissing can go on a long time. Teenagers can do it for hours. The result is swollen, chafed, sometimes even bruised lips. Bitten lips are very sexy. The actress Liv Tyler's lips always look like she's just been deep kissing. They're undeniably part of her sexy goddess appeal.

Shane: *My male friend's lower lip was all chewed up. He does have enticingly full lips! I teased him about it, and he told me it was from the beautiful Greek woman he had begun seeing. He said she really liked to kiss. I laughed in recognition, because I instantly got the picture. Hey, I told him. I'm a bit of a biter myself.*

Here's another kind of lip-biting scenario. You are kissing the other person. He may or may not be your lover—yet, anyway. You are so hot for this person, you're going wild. You are kissing him so hard and he is kissing you back so hard that you're stumbling, you're reeling, you're both peeling clothes off. Your lips are smashing into each other like rough waves against the shore. You are breathing hard through your noses. Your mouths are only torn apart for nanoseconds as you struggle for air. You make the move to take what's happening to the next level. You seize his lower lip between your teeth. You're way beyond gentle nibbling. You're holding his lip firmly between your teeth. You're applying some pressure, but not enough to draw blood. This kissing feels best if your partner has a nice cushy lip, but even thin lips will swell when they are well and thoroughly kissed. Lips are an erogenous zone. Explore them. Kissing is a mirror to cunnilingus. Treat your partner's mouth the way you would like someone else's mouth to treat your vagina and clitoris. The best cunnilingus involves licking, sucking, nibbling, yes, sometimes even slurping. Just as a woman will

climax from excellent cunnilingus, some lucky women can climax
from excellent kissing.

Other Places to Chew On

Other places to put your lips, teeth, and mouth are the throat,
shoulders, breasts, and belly. Many goddesses go wild when they
are lightly bitten along the insides of their thighs. The insides of the
thighs can be an intense erogenous zone, especially when the flesh
is stimulated by a partner's roving, hot mouth. I have experienced
tremendous orgasms as a result of having the insides of my thighs
lightly chewed on. The area is very rich in nerve endings, and being
so close to the genitals, any tingles that begin along the insides of
the thighs are sent directly to the primary nerve center. But the flesh
along the insides of a woman's thighs is usually rather delicate. Be
careful how much pressure you allow your lover to apply there
unless you welcome the black-and-blue look.

The Love Bite

The Kama Sutra describes eight different kinds of biting: the
hidden bite, the swollen bite, the point bite, the line of points bite,
the coral and the jewel, the line of jewels, the broken cloud, and
the biting of the boar. Feeling overwhelmed? Some bites describe
a simple reddening of the skin, while others are more wounding.
Women of different regions of India are described in the text for
their fondness or rejection of different degrees of biting and where
they prefer to be bitten. Although the book was written by a man,
he certainly was no sexist: The Kama Sutra makes it clear that a
woman who has been bitten by a man during an act of passion
should bite back with double force.

Carrie: *I gave my boyfriend a hickey. I was kissing his neck. I guess I
got carried away by the cologne he was wearing—it's my favorite scent.*

While we were kissing, he was running his hands all over my body, making me really hot. I didn't mean to leave a mark on him, but later when we were getting ready to leave the apartment, I saw he had a dark bruise. I told him to wear a scarf or something to cover it, but he just laughed.

Hickeys are caused by a strong sucking action that breaks some of the blood vessels lying just beneath the skin. The area becomes bruised and can become sore and sensitive. The mark usually lasts a few days. The most usual place for a hickey is on the throat, but some lovers bestow them on their partner's breast. There's an old wives' tale that you can get rid of a hickey quickly by pressing a very cold spoon against the mark. That will help reduce swelling, but does nothing to lessen the dark purple color of the bruise. Many goddesses despise and deplore hickeys as being common or trashy. Other goddesses adore them and love flaunting their temporary love tattoos.

Tickle Torture

If biting seems too much for you, what about tickle torture? Many women say their primary erogenous zone is their breasts. Tickling, stroking, teasing the nipples into hardened little points is a lovely form of torture that you don't need to be an S&M princess to enjoy! Many men, by the way, also delight in having their nipples stimulated and dream of their partners biting and pinching them on their chests to enhance their own orgasm. Here's Jamie's personal tickling story.

Jamie: *When I was a kid, my weakness was that I hated being tickled. Naturally, my friends quickly figured this out. I was a victim of their tickling for years. I was always humiliated, because even though I hated their tickling me, part of me also loved it. While it was happening, I would be half crying and screaming, but after they stopped and moved*

*away from me, my panties would always be soaked. For years, as an
adult woman, I seriously avoided being tickled. If any lovers even play-
fully tried to tickle me, I would become extremely upset with them. Eventually the inevitable happened, and one day a lover held me down. He
had me on the floor and was tickling me unmercifully. I cried out and
tried as hard as I could to wriggle away from him, but it was no use. He
kept tickling me and tickling me until I was curled up in a spasm of
misery and pleasure. At first, I was only dimly aware of how aroused I
was. When a wave of orgasmic pleasure washed over me, it took me
totally by surprise. Now I know why I hated my friends' tickling. It was
because their actions gave me so much pleasure, but at the time I was
unaware of what that pleasure really was.*

Love Wrestling

If you've never wrestled with your partner, you're missing out big
time. Wrestling can lead to a powerful orgasm. Real wrestling
should be avoided, however, unless you're both in superb condition, approximately in the same weight class, extremely competi-
tive with each other, and not afraid of getting hurt.

While I don't advise actual boxing-glove sparring for lovers unless
they're both up for it, the kind of wrestling I'm recommending is
really athletic foreplay. Sexual wrestling is best done on a bed. It's
fun to struggle for a bit to see who's going to be on top. If you have
splendid leg muscles, wrestling is a great way to show them off! The
friction created by your two bodies jostling each other, and jockey-
ing for position usually creates its own heat. In an ideal sex tussle,
you'll both be breathing a bit hard and your heart will be pumping.
Your body is already halfway to orgasm. All it takes is a little bit of
sex now to push you over the top. Ava can testify to this.

Ava: *I was astride him, clearly in charge. I was teasing him by pinning
his arms to his sides with my thighs. We were half naked and sweaty.*

We'd just returned from a run. I wasn't really planning on having sex right that minute. I thought that would happen later, in the shower. But he wasn't taking my pinning him lying down. He pulled some slick wrestling move and heaved me off. In a flash, he had me turned over. The next thing I knew, I was face down on the bed and he was pulling my shorts down. I tried kicking him away, but he grabbed my ankles, stopping me. One moment I was laughing and the next I was gasping when he gave my butt a good spank. It startled me, but it also aroused me. He worked his penis in, holding me by one ankle. I struggled for a minute and then just gave up. It felt too good to fight him. I started having an orgasm immediately. I was positively gushing all over him.

Water wrestling can be fun, too.

Ellie: *We were in our pool, fooling around. The kids were in the house asleep, and we were taking a midnight swim. I don't know who started it, but we began dunking each other. I was really going after him, trying to pull him under. He's six-two, and I'm only five feet tall, so it was like a mosquito going after a giraffe—ha, ha. At one point, I had him in a leg lock, sitting on his shoulders with my thighs wrapped around his neck. Somehow he got me turned around, and his face was pushed into my crotch. He started making growling sounds and shaking his head from side to side like a wet dog. All of a sudden, I felt really excited. I grabbed his head and pulled it even closer to me. He instantly got the message, and we got out of the pool. You never saw two people get their bathing suits off so fast. We made it right there on the pool deck on a chaise lounge. We did it missionary position, where it usually takes me a while to come, but this time my orgasm came upon me in a blast. I think it was because of all that rough stuff we were doing in the water.*

Scratching

Scratching is another exciting thing you can do to or with your lover. The Kama Sutra has no less than eleven descriptions for scratching someone. Some of the marks described are the half moon, a circle, a peacock's foot, and the leaf of a blue lotus. Some of these marks require skill to correctly execute. Courtesans throughout history have been well acquainted with a variety of special nail effects.

Modern goddesses may not have at their fingertips the ancient names for love scratches, but that doesn't mean they aren't aware of the sexiness of having long, shapely nails and the effect those nails have on their partners. Here's what manicure fiend Chloe had to say about it:

Chloe: *I admit I am a bit obsessed about getting my nails done. For one thing, I love the back rub they always give you while your nails are drying. But I also love the way my hands look after a manicure. I love my long, shaped, painted nails . . . and my lover loves the way they look and feel too.*

Carmen has other ideas about how to put her pretty nails to good use.

Carmen: *We have a little game that we sometimes play in bed. It definitely involves my manicure. My boyfriend lies naked on the bed while I drag my nails up and down his body. I start around his collarbone and slowly work my way down. I vary the pressure so that sometimes my nails are just tickling, but as the game continues, my scratches become harder. The longer I can draw things out, the better it gets, because the harder his penis becomes. When he's rock hard and his penis is pointing to his navel, he likes me to scratch the shaft ever so lightly. I've discovered he also enjoys a light scratching of his balls. He says he gets off on the appearance of my fingers, since his last girlfriend was a serious gardener and she never, ever got her nails done. I must say that the tiny welts my nails raise on his skin give me a rush. By the time he's ready to enter me, I'm always super wet and hot. The only other time I ever* *scratched anyone was when I was really mad. Come to think of it, I was turned on by that angry scratching, too.*

Films such as *Nine ½ Weeks,* starring Mickey Rourke and Kim Basinger, a love story homage to rough sex, have made a cult out of sex that leaves bruises. This kind of lovemaking is not for everyone. But if you enjoy a bit of rough play or one day (or night) find yourself getting carried away in the moment leaving tell tale marks behind, don't feel guilty about giving free rein to your animalistic instincts. A scratch or two born out of an intense orgasm never hurt anyone . . . and a sexily chewed-up lip is very exciting.

Beyond the Bedroom:
Sex Outdoors, in Cars,
Anywhere but the Bed

*N*aturally, a goddess is most comfortable where she feels safest, which is usually in her own bedroom. It's where she's most likely to experience her best orgasms, although I've had some pretty tasty ones just sitting at my desk, in the middle of the day, looking out a window. I call my little desk matinee orgasms the "pause that refreshes," because it really does freshen me up.

Comfort preferences and security issues aside, every goddess worth her weight in gold has had mind-blowing, knocked-senseless orgasms in alternative locales. By alternative I mean not the bed, not the bedroom, not even the shower, because having sex in the bathtub and/or the shower should be so basic to you that it cannot possibly be conceived as alternative. If for some reason you are not already pleasuring yourself somehow in the bathroom— and I include soaping yourself thoroughly with your favorite scented soap to be pleasuring—go in the bathroom right now, and as my goddess friend Giovanna says, "whack off!" As for sex outside the perimeters of your boudoir and private lavatory, consider what Vanessa had to say on the topic.

Vanessa: *Once you've been married for many years, it's the unexpected places to have sex that are sexy, not the same (fucking) bedroom. Like in a car parked by a reservoir late at night. Or maybe a cheap motel. Or outside in a public park after it gets dark.*

You should go out and have sex someplace different. You can only enhance and educate your sexual palate by appreciating and sampling a range of experiences. Why limit yourself to always making love in the same bed, room, street, city, even country? Fabulous sex and sexy experiences—and orgasms!—are to be had everywhere, even when you only hear about them.

A True Sexy Story

This sexy situation happened so far from my usual sex haunts that I wasn't even present. My muse told me this story one morning over coffee. He had just come from riding a commuter train from the city after spending an erotic evening with one of his city girlfriends. In the morning, they rode the subway uptown so she could go to work and he could get to the train station. The train was crowded, and they had to stand very close together. Pressed up against one another after a full night of love, their bodies were melting into each other even through winter clothing. She was wearing a skirt, and he managed to slide his hand up her leg and into her pantyhose to touch her pussy. That's all he did—touched her very privately in a very public place. I instantly remembered when I was riding the subways myself how, even though it could be unbearably hot and claustrophobic, the very anonymity and the speeding motion of the train were undeniably sexy. His words sent an electrifying pulse surging through me. They gave me a vicarious thrill, certainly something juicy to file away in my mental treasure trove of fabulous fantasy sex.

Try some of these "not the bedroom" locations inspired by the correspondents to spice up your sex life.

Make Love in the Kitchen

Chloe: *It all started when he said he couldn't wait to get me in the kitchen. He meant when we would start cooking together, but I don't cook! I told my girlfriend about it, because this is a new boyfriend and that's all we talk about: my sex life. She said, Don't worry. Just make love to him in the kitchen, let him cook for you, and it will all work out. So I did it. I gave him head in the kitchen. He leaned back against the sink, and I dropped into a squat (good thing I've kept up with my leg exercises) and unzipped his zipper. His penis—and this guy is forty-two—sprang out at me like a teenager's. It was pretty exciting, seeing him jump to attention that way. It takes a bit longer for him to get that hard in bed. I started out licking him, and then I started sucking. He wound his hands in my hair and started rubbing my neck. My neck is very sensitive, so him rubbing and stroking it while I was blowing him felt really good to me. Really good. When I first started sucking him, I thought it would be just the warm-up, but for some reason I started getting deep into it. It was like I didn't want to stop. I don't know if it was the oddness of being in the kitchen or just that we mostly had all our clothes on, his pants around his knees and my sweater pushed up for him to see my breasts and my bra, or how good it felt with him rubbing my neck—no kidding, I am a real neck fanatic—but I decided to go all the way. Take him to the limit. I felt myself getting wetter and wetter. My clit was so hard! I touched myself and I was soaking wet. I just squeezed my pussy a little bit and kept on sucking. The next thing I knew, we were both coming. It was pretty wild. I finally found a good use for my kitchen.*

It's Not Called the "Great Outdoors" for Nothing

Shane says you don't have to be a woodswoman to become one with nature, especially if hiking, mountain climbing, or canoe trips are not your thing. You can have a love connection anywhere in the open air—even in the backyard.

Shane: *A while ago, I joined a group of women who said they were practicing Wiccans. I'm still not really sure what Wicca is. I know it's a religion, and it has a lot of rituals, and some of them include nakedness. The women invited me to join them for a naked midnight ceremony in someone's private garden. I was curious about it. I was going through an experimental phase of my life. I was what you might call a seeker. I still am! Anyway, it was a beautiful garden and, as promised, very private. First, we drank wine. Then they said some Wiccan prayers or incantations. Then we really did take off all our clothes and danced in the moonlight. Did I mention it was a full moon? Here was a surprising thing. When they had their clothes on, I didn't think some of the women were all that attractive, but naked, they were glowing! It might have been the moonlight. I'm not a lesbian, but I found myself becoming aroused. All those breasts and bottoms bouncing . . . how could I not respond? I was a bit unprepared when two of the women started kissing. Nobody else was really paying much attention, but I was riveted. It was really work for me to turn away.*

A few minutes later, the woman whose house it was asked me to accompany her inside to bring out food she had prepared for the ladies. Inside, I said I had to use the bathroom. Behind the locked door, I thought about those two women kissing and I frigged myself off violently. I almost never penetrate myself when I masturbate. I focus all my attention on the area right beneath my clitoris, which when I'm aroused is like a soft swollen sinkhole of molten desire. But this time, I shoved two fingers inside and pushed myself to the brink really fast. It was all over in two minutes, which is just about the same time I would have taken to use the bathroom. I washed my fingers off really carefully, using some lavender-scented soap she had. If I wasn't going to be handling food, I probably wouldn't have washed my hand. It would have been a turn-on for me and kept up the level of my arousal if I had been able to sniff my pussy-scented fingertips for the rest of the evening.

Take Advantage of an Empty Bedroom
at a Party

Sometimes you have to just respond when opportunity knocks. That's what Leslie did.

Leslie: *I was high, but I definitely was not drunk. We were at a party. All night long, this man kept flirting with me, and it was making me excited. I've been married three years, and the sex is still good, although maybe not as exciting as it once was. It was a dancing party, and I was dancing. My husband does not dance. I was dancing with my sister and one of her friends. There were a few couples on the floor, but mostly it was just women dancing. My husband was watching me. He was smiling. He enjoys seeing me having a good time. Then the man who kept flirting with me joined in. He came right up and started dancing with me. At first it was a fast number, but then there was a slow one. We got kind of close. When the song ended, he leaned over and kissed my cheek.*

A few minutes later, my husband grabbed my hand and led me down the hall and into an empty bedroom. We started making out. Then we were lying on the bed. I didn't even know if the door was locked. He pushed up my skirt and pulled down my panties. He started fingering me and kissing me at the same time. I was so wet. I touched his penis, and he was rock hard and throbbing. He whispered in my ear, "That guy wants to fuck you, and that makes me want to fuck you." He pushed himself inside me and we started. I was so wet, he could thrust hard right away. The dancing and the flirting had got me all juiced up. I hooked my legs around his lower hips and leaned back on my elbows, half sitting up. The angle of penetration was amazing. I kept my eyes open, because I wanted to watch him working away at me. I also was looking around the room, which was wild because obviously it was a young person's bedroom. There were movie and music posters stuck with pushpins on the walls. It felt so decadent, so dangerous, to be having sex there. Any moment, anyone could have walked in the room. But no one did, and we went on like that for a long time. Gradually, I just zeroed in on what was going on between us, and the party down the hall seemed very far away. When I came, it was a long, slow, vaginal orgasm, the kind that makes your whole body spasm and your belly contract. I could actually feel my uterus vibrating. When we got home about two hours later, we made love again. It was good, but nothing as intense as what I had just experienced.

Empty Road. Sunday Drive. Why Not "Do It in the Road?"

When she leased her new car, Christine didn't realize that breathtaking orgasms were part of the deal.

Christine: *We were taking a Sunday drive. I had just gotten a new car, a little red Miata convertible. My boyfriend was with me. It was a gorgeous day, warm enough to have the top down. My hair was whipping around, I was playing Bonnie Raitt, and we were laughing and having a great time. He was teasing me, playing with me while I was driving, reaching across to rub my thigh and squeezing my hand when I had it on the gearshift. At one point, he grabbed my hand and put it on his erection, which was practically poking a hole in his jeans. It was too big and insistent to ignore for very long, so I pulled over. Since the roads were practically deserted, I went down on him. I didn't get to finish the job, because someone was coming. Even though we were inside the car and they probably would have just driven past, it threw me off. I started the car again and got back on the road.*

A couple of miles later, we saw a sign for a scenic outlook and my boyfriend told me to stop. We both got out of the car to admire the view. My boyfriend started hugging me and got me in a liplock. He put my hand back on his penis, which was really big and throbbing. "You've got to help me out with this," he said, kind of growling. He turned me around and bent me over the hood of my Miata. He pulled my jeans and my panties down over my hips and touched me between my legs. I got wet immediately. He used some of my moisture to wet his cock. He put the head of it right at the mouth of my vagina and pushed. It went right in. He banged me right there on the road over the hood of my car. I was gasping. I was really hot. At that moment, I wouldn't have cared if a carload of state troopers or the road patrol showed up. I arched my back and pushed my bottom right up against him to meet every thrust. I don't think it went on too long. I was coming and coming. Because he hadn't put on a condom, he pulled out before the moment of truth and spurted all over my lower back. Luckily, I had some tissues in the glove compartment that we could use to clean up. We got back in the car and drove straight to the next place we saw that sold beer. For some reason, I was really thirsty afterward, and a beer was all I could think about. That, and the next time I could have sex on the hood of my Miata.

House Hunting? Make Use of an Empty One

Again, sometimes you just have to take advantage of a fortuitous situation. Camille did.

Camille: *My husband and I were looking at real estate. We saw one house three times. The real estate agent was getting sick of showing it to us, I could tell. When I called her to ask if we could see it just one more time, she said go see it yourself. She made a special arrangement. My husband said he'd come by on his lunch break for one more look. I never intended for us to start making love in the house, but that's what happened. I was inspecting the laundry room when he arrived. He started kissing me against the dryer. First it was just kissing, and then he undid my blouse. The next thing, I was sitting on top of the dryer, and he was between my legs, nuzzling me. He worked with his tongue for a long time. It was incredibly exciting, because this is not something he usually does. I was crying out with pleasure and grinding my crotch into his* mouth. *I could not get enough of his tongue. He had one finger inside me and another on my clit and his tongue was just swirling around and around. I felt faint and dizzy, but at the same time I had never felt so alive. I came in his mouth. Liquid was just pouring out of me. My husband got a big shit-eating grin on his face. "I guess this is the right house," he said. We called the real estate agent right afterward and made our offer. The funny thing is, the whole time we were waiting for the closing and to move in, I couldn't stop thinking about our sexy scene in the laundry room.*

An Unfamiliar Motel Room Can Be Electrifying

Women's advice magazines and romantic fiction suggest that vacation sex is the best sex there is. My own experiences in regard to vacation sex is that I always expect too much. Vacation sex can mean a lot of pressure. You're in a room you paid a lot of money for. You want to have amazing sex just to get your money's worth! But the first night, you eat too-rich food for dinner or you have too much to drink or you're jet-lagged or travel fatigued. You can have amazing sex with your partner on a vacation, but my advice is don't try to do anything the first night. The best thing to do the first night is get some sleep.

Shane: *The few times I've forced myself to have sex the first night of vacation, it hasn't been too great. Maybe it's because of all the anticipation, especially if you and your partner have really been looking forward to the trip. Now I've learned that you should deliberately abstain from sex the first night you get anywhere. Have a nice dinner. Take a swim if you can. Relax. When you get into bed, you should just cuddle. By the morning, you'll be feeling fresh and randy. That's a good time to make love. That's when you can really take the time to appreciate each other and the wonderful new place you're in. Plus, you can make love in the bed and also in the bathroom. Vacation bathrooms always have fun* *things in them that you probably don't have at home, like a bidet, for example. You can have an orgasm on a bidet, you know. You just keep the water squirting exactly where you want it. Even if you don't come from it, it's a helluva way to get warmed up. My dream vacation includes sex at least twice a day: first thing in the morning and then again maybe in the afternoon, sometime before dinner, actually. I like making love in the afternoons on vacation, because in my regular life I never get the chance for afternoon sex. When you're on vacation, you can have long lovemaking sessions that take all afternoon and then take a nap together afterward. That leaves you refreshed for dinner and all the fun things you might do later in the evening. Then if you've had a lot to drink or you feel too full from a rich dessert, there's no pressure to make love again before you go to sleep. You wake up rested and you don't have to go anywhere. When I'm on vacation, I like to knock off a couple of orgasms even before I have my first cup. Of coffee, I mean. Also, when you're on vacation you don't have to worry about making a mess of the sheets.*

PART V

The Big O

In the end, it's all about release.

—Goddess motto

Is Any Special Time
of the Month Better for
Having an Orgasm?

*W*hether you're a young nymph just entering your fertility phase, a twenty-, thirty- or forty-year-old woman with or without children, or a fully mature goddess in menopause, there is no reason why you can't enjoy a rousing burst of an orgasm at any time of the month. The nature of feminine physiology is that our bodies are engineered so that orgasm is not tied to ovulation or menstrual cycle. What this means is you can engage in sex or pleasure yourself at any time and get full satisfaction from your efforts!

For Erica, desire is linked to her menstrual cycle.

Erica: *Days one through five of my period, I'm generally tired, achy, and "messy." By the time day seven comes rolling around, I'm generally over my period and feeling much better. For the next seven days (seven through fourteen) I know I'm at my peak, sexually. My senses seem to be more acute and, in general, I feel a lot more amorous. The orgasms can be incredibly intense and long during this time frame. That feeling gradually fades from days fifteen through twenty-two, but if in the right mood with the right person, I'm feeling very good. A couple of days before my period, I feel a bit more stressed, but that's nothing that some good loving won't cure.*

Is there any clinical evidence that a woman is more likely to have an orgasm at a particular point in her cycle? It's difficult to say.

According to Gabrielle Lichterman, a journalist on women's health issues, women are more likely to orgasm at ovulation when their estrogen and testosterone levels rise. She said it is because the hormones released at these times naturally heighten a woman's interest in sex and make lubrication easier. It's hardly a new thought. Eighty years ago, another journalist, Frank Harris, editor of *The Saturday Review* and author of *My Life and Loves*, a classic volume of politics and erotica published in 1925, quoted from the work of Dr. Marie Carmichael Stopes, then-president of the Society for Constructive Birth Control. Her 1923 book, *Contraception: Its Theory, History and Practice*, indicated that there are two or three days in each monthly period when a woman is most likely to be eager in her response to physical love. Harris commented on Stopes' theories in his renowned memoir of politics, literature, and lovemaking, because it was his personal observation—after making love to literally hundreds of women—that just before a woman's period, "when the vitality of her seed is departing," was when he found his partners to be orgasmic. "The two best moments of the month I have found to be just before the period and about the eighth or ninth day after the period has ceased," Harris wrote in his book, "although I may be of course mistaken. Pioneers seldom find the best road and the spiritual factors of every human being are infinitely more important than the merely animal." Harris also thought that spring and autumn were optimal seasons for women to enjoy making love. He wrote, "One of the most difficult things to find out in the majority of women is the time they are most easily excited and most apt to the sexual act. Some few are courageous enough to tell their lover when they really want him, but usually he has to find the time and the season for himself."

Decades after Harris published his anthropological musings, most men and women are still in the dark connecting orgasm and desire to any calendar! I asked the goddesses in my circle if they noticed any connection to their sexual appetite and their menstrual cycle, or if they were no longer menstruating what affect it had on their ability to orgasm. This is what they said.

Bella finds that she is especially horny and orgasmic just before her period.

Bella: *The day or the night before I get my period, there's an insanity that comes over me that makes me incredibly horny. I always, always want to have sex then and I always, always come quickly, powerfully, sometimes several times.*

Shane also is incredibly horny just before her period.

Shane: *A few days before my period, I always feel pretty randy. I find myself touching myself often throughout the day even if I don't have the time or the opportunity to masturbate. If I have a partner, I will definitely take advantage of him! I've yet to meet the man who objects to being used as a tool just because I'm burning up from some hormonal thing.*

Mid-cycle is when Ava finds herself in the mood for lovemaking. This is actually "Nature's Way," because that's when most women are ovulating.

Ava: *I am very horny in the middle of my cycle, which is, of course, when I'm most likely to get pregnant. I already have one child as a result of responding to my need for sex during the middle of my cycle, so now I'm very cautious. Not that I avoid sex when I'm probably ovulating, but I stick to oral sex if I'm with my husband. Otherwise, I just satisfy myself by myself. That's what fingers are for.*

During my own high school and college years, I noticed that I felt more sexual urges, sometimes even wild cravings, in the middle of my menstrual cycle. I am sure this is because female biology is set up this way in order to perpetuate the species. But I also noticed a very strong urge for sex just before my period. As I got older and paid closer attention to the workings of my body, I realized I was often very horny right before my period as well. Sometimes to "bring my period on," I would initiate sex with my partner and engage in vigorous lovemaking. It was always gratifying to me to go to the bathroom after making love and see a tiny spot of red on the toilet tissue. It was evidence to me that intense and energetic love-making resulting in a strong orgasm "did something" to bring my period on. Later, when I married, my partner got used to these strong urges that came upon me just before my period. He was always happy to seize the opportunity, since he knew that once my period began, I would want to abstain from sex for several days.

Many Women Say Their Orgasm Is Linked to Their Hormonal Levels

Helaine says she is at the mercy of her hormones and artificially induced estrogen.

Helaine: *I differ on when I want it and when I don't. My body is inconsistent! I think it's because I'm on birth control pills, so the estrogen gods are controlling me. I want to have sex the first day I'm off them, and that's a good thing because it's always a Sunday, and my husband and I can shove our child off somewhere so we can grab an hour or so to be alone.*

Orgasm and PMS

Some women who suffer from PMS or mild to moderate premenstrual cramps say they want to make love shortly before their periods, because their orgasms relieve some of their PMS and cramping symptoms. A number of the correspondents reported that orgasm reduces their menstrual cramps and cuts down on other menstrual-related complaints, such as crankiness, lethargy, and the sensation of feeling chilled. Jolie deliberately uses orgasm to alleviate her severe menstrual cramps caused by endometriosis, a chronic, painful condition in which abnormal tissue, similar to the tissue that lines the uterus (endometrium) grows in the abdomen and elsewhere in the body. It causes internal bleeding, inflammation, scarring, severe pain, and fatigue, and sometimes infertility. The condition worsens over time, although it is almost never fatal. It can be treated with pain medication, hormones, and surgery.

Jolie: *Ever since my teens when I was diagnosed with endometriosis and read about orgasms helping with cramps, I've masturbated to orgasm for pain relief almost every month, until I had a baby, which "cures" endometriosis.*

In the past, Guilianna also used her orgasms to serve a medicinal and palliative purpose.

Guilianna: *I do sometimes wank (my preferred term for masturbation) if I have period cramps, which now that I am fifty-one are rare. But I used to have to have an orgasm to relieve the pain and stop the cramps. It was kind of like defibrillating my uterus—stopping the cramps by having rhythmic orgasm contractions.*

Prohibitions Against Intercourse During Menstruation

There are many prohibitions against intercourse during menstruation. The Koran specifically says "No Way!" to it. In the Orthodox Jewish faith, a menstruating woman is considered "unclean," and her husband is forbidden to engage in sexual relations with her until she has taken the ritual "mikvah" bath. There is a substantial body of medical literature warning about the dangers of engaging in intercourse while a woman is bleeding. A study conducted by

Dr. Winnifred Cutler of the Athena Institute for Women's Wellness in Chester Springs, Pennsylvania, revealed that engaging in coitus during menstruation has been associated with heavier bleeding patterns in perimenopausal women (women who are going through the transitional phase from normal menstrual periods to no periods at all) whose median age was forty-eight years old. Perimenopause, for the record, can go on for years. Dr. Cutler's findings, which were published in the *Journal of Psychosomatic Obstetrics and Gynecology* in 1996, connected the high rate of hysterectomies in this country to women reporting these heavier bleeding patterns to their physicians, who in turn recommended the surgery.

Yet there are women who enjoy intercourse with their partners during their periods. Helaine is one of them. So is Chloe.

Helaine: *I have a great orgasm while I'm having my period—it is more of a physical release to me, but then anticipating the mess afterwards sometimes puts me off. My husband, by the way, shares none of my fastidiousness.*

Chloe: *When I know I am just about to get my period, I've noticed that a good bout of intercourse always seems to bring it on sooner, sometimes by hours, sometimes by even a day. On those occasions, orgasm can always happen. And if I have a partner who doesn't mind the bloody mess of a period, I've learned that my orgasm can really alleviate menstrual cramps! Beats taking Midol any day.*

Sela used to make love with her husband while she was bleeding, although she has since given up the practice.

Sela: *My husband and I used to engage in something he nicknamed "Vampire Sex," because of all the blood. I know it sounds kinky, but we both really got into it. I've had some of the most amazing orgasms of my life while I've been having my period. I can't explain it. I feel fuller,* *more aroused, it seems like every erogenous zone is extra sensitive, super pumped up. My breasts are fuller, my genitals are already swollen, the blood, gross as this sounds, acts as an extra lubricant. I was really disappointed when the doctor of Chinese medicine I see told me to stop doing it. She said it could lead to vaginal infections. So we stopped. But I do have fond and exciting memories of doing it before we knew better.*

Kendra speculates that she got a vaginal infection from having sex during her period.

Kendra: *I don't have sex when I'm on my period anymore. I did it a few times, and it gave me a vaginal infection, which I typically don't get. My rule now is I don't let any penises near me when I'm bleeding. I think it's nature's way of telling you to take some time out.*

Avoid Intercourse, but Go for the Orgasm

It probably is a good idea to avoid actual intercourse while you are having your period, but that doesn't mean you have to forego your orgasm. If you are feeling aroused and want to bring yourself to orgasm by masturbating, alone or with your partner, go ahead. During sexual stimulation, your body becomes excited as your blood pressure, breathing, and heart rate increase. The blood vessels in the genital area fill with blood, causing an enlargement of the clitoris. The labia swell, and vaginal secretions sometimes go into overdrive. As your excitement level peaks, a muscular tension fills your entire body until the moment of your climax, when excitement and pleasure push you over the edge into orgasm. When the body stiffens and the muscles involuntarily squeeze and contract, the body experiences spasms in different areas, not just the genitals, but your arms, your legs, your back, even your neck. The muscles of the vagina seize and release rapidly, as does the uterus. Bartholin's glands, which are responsible for lubricating the vagina, discharge a watery secretion. Immediately after orgasm, endorphins are released into the body. You may have heard about endorphins, but still not know what they are. Endorphins are the substances naturally formed and released into the body to relieve pain. When enough of them are released into the body, they can even make you feel high. Endorphins are also partly responsible for regulating the hormonal system. The goddess advice is that you should have as many orgasms as you like even if you have your period. Orgasms are good for you. They warm you up, stimulate the circulatory system, relieve tension and stress. And if they make your cramps go away, so much the better.

Menopause Makes a Difference

Menopause, of course, changes the picture. When you've stopped menstruating, there is never a "wrong time." But many women report a marked decrease in interest in sex after menopause, mostly because of vaginal dryness and night sweats. While a study undertaken by the University of Pennsylvania reported that sixty percent of the women participating in the study said they experienced a decrease in sexual desire after menopause, the same study showed that hormone replacement therapy was considered "good for sex," because it relieved many of the physically uncomfortable symptoms associated with menopause. But no studies have been done to gauge the impact of hormone replacement therapy on a woman's sex drive, which Dr. Barbara Bartlik, an assistant professor at Weill Medical College of Cornell University called "annoying." Anecdotal evidence from the women responding to *The Goddess Orgasm* survey revealed that some women find that menopause and the lack of messy periods made sex liberating. Roxanne is one of them.

Roxanne: *I have found menopause to be completely and totally liberating to my sex life. Of course, my body isn't quite what it used to be in* *terms of muscle tone, but my mind is sooooooo completely open now to almost anything. Not having my period anymore has truly been a freeing experience!*

Many women who feel their sex life is over after menopause are responding less to lack of desire than to symptoms. Vaginal dryness is the principal one. Dryness can be combated with vaginal moisturizers, gels, and creams. There are many personal lubricants on the market, many of which can be bought over the counter in any drugstore. Among these are K-Y Liquid, Vagisil Intimate Lubricant, and Astroglide. Vaginal moisturizers such as Replens, Moist Again, and K-Y Long Lasting are popular over-the-counter brands. Products that contain estrogen must be gotten through a doctor, since they are prescription only. Several worth asking for include Premarin Cream and Estrace Cream. There are also prescription-only vaginal tablets like Vagifem and vaginal rings like the Femring and the Estring, containing estrogen, also available only by prescription. Be aware that, as with any medication containing estrogen, the hormone is absorbed into the bloodstream and can affect breast and uterine health. Ask your doctor if any of these medications is right for you.

The Most Auspicious Time to Experience Orgasm: Is Nighttime the Right Time?

$\mathcal{I}$s there a best time of day—or night—to have an orgasm? Are some hours or moments more propitious than others for harnessing your special power and ultimately bringing it off? As a female who has experienced orgasm at just about every time of day and night—and yes, even in my sleep!—I can say with some authority that there is no right or wrong time of day to pleasure yourself or make love. Surges of orgasmic pleasure can be produced at any time.

Any moment the urge or the opportunity to have an orgasm strikes, you should savor it. While any goddess worthy of the name can arouse herself any time, most goddesses, even young novice goddesses in training, can benefit from listening to their bodies to hear what that body has to say.

Many women, especially young and fecund ones, wake up in a semi-aroused state. The most positive proof of evidence of this that you can discover for yourself is to slip one finger between your legs the moment you open your eyes. What you are doing is monitoring your moisture level. If you are wet, you are ready. Ready for what is your choice. Will it be a quickie encounter with the handheld shower attachment for a Wake Me Up orgasm . . . or a long lazy roll in the sheets with your partner? Orgasms frequently happen easily first thing in the morning, because even if the mind is not fully functioning, the body is awake. Orgasms can sneak up fast on you first thing in the morning, because you're still in the grip of an erotic dream, or because you've been blessed by waking up next to a partner whose hard erection is only waiting for the touch of your fingertips.

Joy in the Morning

As a rule, men usually wish to engage in sex in the morning. And no wonder—men have the physiological advantage of waking up aroused. The majority of men, even older, less virile ones, wake up with an erection. If they are fortunate enough to be reclining beside a goddess, they want to take advantage of it. Will you or won't you? That is the goddess option.

Taryn: *I like to have sex when I first wake up. Either in the morning or right after a nap.*

Making love or masturbating first thing in the morning can be wonderful. Many women enjoy waking up to the act of love. And why not? You're already soft and pliant and in a dreamlike state. Your body is warm from a night wrapped in bedclothes. The harsh realities of the day ahead are still vague blurs on the mental horizon. The physical body is languorous, fluid, even porous. The voices in our heads, the self-imposed mental barriers that get in the way of orgasm are down.

Serena feels sensuous in the morning, too.

Serena: *I'm a morning person. Morning is the most intense time of day for me. My head is clear and I haven't had any wine yet.*

Early morning sex can be slow and easy (especially if you don't have to leap out of bed to be somewhere), but it can also be quick and efficient. For goddesses who prefer to get their days rolling with a rousing orgasm, ten minutes with a partner, their own hands, or a vibrator is a delightful way to jump-start the day. Many women find orgasm to be invigorating. For those goddesses who have taught their bodies to enjoy a hard, fast, unemotional release where the clitoris is firmly stimulated and orgasm is quickly achieved, there is no better way to start the day. Orgasm is known to be a great reliever of stress; if the day ahead is expected to be exhausting (imagine a full day of meetings, a job interview, a scheduled encounter with someone difficult, such as one's boss), beginning it with orgasmic release is akin to girding one's loins for the battle ahead.

Erica's schedule for the best time to make love changed after she became a mom.

Erica: *I prefer making love at night, but now that I'm married and our kids are older, it's too hard to stay up later than they do. We usually have sex in the morning, which is my partner's favorite time.*

A reluctance to make love in the morning is mostly a time-sensitive issue relating to rigid schedules or a basic hygiene thing. Most women open their eyes only to fix them immediately on the clock. They've allowed themselves fifteen minutes to hop in the shower or to get the kids' breakfasts started up. Or if time is not the issue, "morning mouth" is. They would make love if only they first had a chance to slip into the bathroom to brush their teeth! Morning mouth is a reality. It's true that kissing even your beloved partner first thing in the morning may not be the most appetizing thing, but there are other places than the mouth to kiss. A very goddess-like way to handle this situation is to start the kissing at the navel, then work your way up or down. By the time the eroge-nous zones have been stimulated, stale breath is the last thing on your mind.

You Don't Have to Be Menopausal to Experience Dryness in the Morning

One common objection to early morning sex is that many women complain of being dry in the morning. A dry vagina is not an orgasm maker. Morning dryness is often due to the long hours of sleep when the body is not taking in water. Upon wakening, the body is often dehydrated. Some common medications, such as those prescribed for hypertension and allergy, also leach moisture from the body. Dehydration is the antithesis of desire, which is why it's a good idea for goddesses to keep a carafe of water and a glass by their beds to sip throughout the night. Don't worry about losing sleep while you drink. You probably won't even remember slaking your thirst, but the carafe will be empty by the morning.

Morning Sex Isn't Right for Everyone, but It Can Be Nice to Be Persuaded

Some very high-powered goddesses, however, are real efficiency experts. Anything that throws their routines off in the morning is just "off" for them.

Chelsea: *I like making love most times, but not first thing in the morning. I have a routine that I stick to that doesn't include sex in the mornings. Instead, it's coffee, taking out the dogs, showering, checking e-mail, and breakfast.*

For others, a variation in the routine is not always unwelcome. You might not be in the mood to make love with your partner first thing in the morning, but once in a while it pays to respond to a randy bedmate's wishes. Carole was.

Carole: *I never feel I'm in the mood for morning sex, but on occasion I've been talked into it, and it turned out to be great anyway!*

Afternoon Delight

A strong urge to slip your fingers in your panties may come over you in the middle of the workday. Goddesses have been known to furiously bring themselves off in the lavatories of their offices, especially if it's the day after a long night of love. In the aftermath of a major orgasm, aftershocks have a way of creeping up on you until nothing will do except to have another one. Betty Dodson, the diva of masturbation, recommends self-pleasuring breaks throughout the day, much the way somebody less inventive might recommend coffee breaks. Think about it. Instead of refueling yourself with caffeine and sugar, you could be rubbing your thighs together until there is an inescapable desire to fondle your clitoris to refresh and invigorate yourself instead. Shocked? Don't put the idea down till you try it. Helaine did.

Helaine: *I love afternoon sex! Nighttime sex is too demanding (there's this feeling that you've got to), and mornings do not interest me at all!*

Guilianna also described herself as an afternoon person.

Giulianna: *Afternoon delight. That's my thing. Especially if sun is streaming in through the window.*

Afternoons Are a Great Time to Self-Pleasure

Afternoons are actually one of the best times for getting in touch with yourself for a masturbation session. Imagine you've got an entire afternoon alone. No errands to run. No appointments to keep. It's just you and your favorite motion-lotion, or that hot novel with the spicy passages, or even an adult film you rented but haven't yet dared to watch. Maybe your desire has been momentarily inflamed by someone you ran into on the street or the recollection of an old flame who was well versed in how to light you up. Reverie is the best place to begin for an afternoon of self-indulgence. It's so much healthier for you than devouring a box of chocolates. To begin, make yourself comfortable, unfasten your trousers, loosen your bra, remove any restricting garments and prepare to send yourself into The Zone. Carla tried it.

Carla: *One afternoon coming home from work, I was driving past a construction site. I saw the most amazing looking cop standing in an intersection. Just driving by him and looking at him made me feel light-headed, as though I were going to pass out! The sight of him flooded me with erotic thoughts and feelings. Mind you, this was the middle of the day, and all I had exchanged with him was one glance! Luckily, I was almost home. I took care of business the moment I got there. There was really nothing else I could do. I was so hot that I had no choice but to get myself off! That was years ago, but I still savor the orgasm and the experience. Instant arousal—is there anything better?*

Shane enjoys pleasuring herself midday when there's nobody around.

Shane: *When I was a nymph, a young goddess coming up, the mood to pleasure myself could come over me at the most unusual moments. I didn't even have to be particularly horny. Sometimes lying on the sofa in a fit of youthful boredom, I'd be reading a book, sometimes even one for school, and something I would read would trigger in me such an intense erotic impulse or summon up such a vivid fantasy that I would have to immediately send my fingers between my legs. I was amazed at how quickly and out of nowhere I might suddenly become wet. I confess my preferred reading matter always contained some steamy passages, and some of my favorite books (many of them the great classics) became dog-eared and frayed. But the sensual sensations that washed over me and compelled me to put down whatever I was doing in order to mas-turbate could and did occur at almost any time of day. Other times, these urges might be triggered by a strong wave of sunlight, like the bright sunlight at high noon on a sandy beach, or from the sweat I'd work up doing an hour of chores in the yard.*

Samantha likes to take advantage of a quiet house.

Samantha: *When I'm pleasuring myself, when it's quiet at home and the need hits, I'm a daytime girl. Otherwise, with a partner, it's generally in the evening or late at night, sometimes very early in the morning. There is no "has to be" time for making love. It's more according to our work and social schedules—when I can fit sex in. Although most of the men I've been with wake up "ready," and if they can rouse me from my sleep, whether it's an afternoon nap or the crack of dawn, I'm game.*

One of my own favorite afternoon delights always spontaneously occurs when I unexpectedly discover myself home alone. Silence has often been enough to arouse me, especially since my home is usually filled with a cacophony of diverting sounds, not all of them conducive to the orgasmic experience. You really have to possess superhuman goddessy powers to be able to tune out blaring televisions, banging drums, jackhammers, the constant opening and shutting of doors. Men, of course, can be relied on to have sex under the most turbulent conditions, including barking dogs and crying infants. Women customarily need a quiet time to focus, which is why an empty house in the afternoon is the perfect place. Jamie likes to give vent to her favorite oral sex fantasies if she finds herself alone in the middle of the day.

Jamie: *Oral sex is one of my enduring masturbatory fantasies. Over the years, I have discovered my capacity to enjoy it in real time, but in the flesh it rarely compares to the orgasms I can give myself through an imagined oral sex fantasy. My partners in my fantasy frequently change, and they are seldom people I can imagine sharing such intimacies with in real life. Very often they come under the category of "forbidden fruit," which means they might be the spouse of a friend or the bearded, scruffy guy who pumped gas for me at the station. In my mind, I construct the flimsiest of situations to throw me and this individual together, although*

I have been known to dispense with any kind of plotline whatsoever to simply hurl myself into a masturbatory frenzy, especially if time is limited. In real life, I sometimes become anxious while receiving oral sex, because the sight of my partner's face between my legs, staring up at me, gauging the progress of my pleasure, is disconcerting. In my fantasy of receiving lavish oral sex, I never look down.

Is Nighttime the Right Time?

One real advantage, not to mention convenience, of making love or masturbating at night when you are already in bed is that you have disrobed, if you are not in fact actually naked. Making love at night has many advantages leading to orgasm. You're lying down. You have easy access to your breasts and your vagina. Should you be sharing your bed, couch, or divan with a consort, chances are they are buck naked, too, and they most assuredly have access to your ready-to-be-awakened flesh. Nothing could be simpler than for one of you to start the process of kissing, licking, stroking, and penetrating that will ultimately lead to a climax. Here's what Elizabeth, Carole, Suzette, and Chloe had to say.

Elizabeth: *I like nighttime.*

Carole: *Nighttime works for me.*

Suzette: *I'm a nighttime girl. I'm not much of a morning person.*

Chloe: *My favorite time of day to make love is in the middle of the night. The element of surprise. If I am dead asleep, I just like the attack. I don't want long foreplay then, but I find the orgasm more intense when I feel my partner just could not sleep without having sex with me. I don't really have a preference for the time of day or night with the vibrator.*

The nighttime orgasm is often perceived as a prelude to sleep. It's the reason so many women count on it to work on them like a tranquilizer. For women whose orgasms are very intense and exhaustive, nighttime orgasm is the most desirable because of its soporific effect. But for women who find orgasm to be energizing and invigorating, experiencing a major climax in the final hours of the evening or the earliest hours of the dawn will cause them to be awake for hours, alert and completely sleepless. If this is true for you, avoid late-night orgasms.

However, waking up in the middle of the night to pleasure oneself or receive someone else's caress is a whole other story. Middle of the night sex is, for Carla, the most pleasurable and intense.

Carla: *If pressed for what time of day do I love sex the most, I would say waking up in the middle of the night and giving myself pleasure is the best.*

Masturbation in the Middle of the Night

Pleasuring yourself in the middle of the night is a unique experience. The arousal itself seems so effortless, so spontaneous. There is none of that slow build that in its own right can be exquisite, but that can also be a source of anxiety or pressure if performance is involved. Middle of the night sex is excellent because it's rarely about performance. It's not about how long you can last or how hard you can ride or what your thighs look like or if you've got jelly-belly. At the point you are awake enough to yearn to masturbate or turn to your partner to engage in the act of love, the body is already in a state of sexual alertness. The pump, to put it bluntly, has been primed. Stroke your own loins in the middle of the night when you awaken from a fevered sex dream, and you will always discover a moistness, a deep well of wetness. In many cases, you will find yourself drenched. Self-induced middle of the night orgasms can be explosive, and they often come on fast.

When Opportunity Knocks, Grab It

Say you're in the middle of the supermarket and you've got a full cart. Suddenly, incongruously, you feel the area between your legs becoming moist and hot. Shivers of pre-orgasmic excitement are already coursing through your body. You wonder what set it off. Was it handling all those cucumbers? You're really hot and bothered, but you can't imagine how you can take care of that. For starters, you're fully dressed, and the idea of loading all these groceries into the trunk of your car and driving home to peel off your pantyhose or jeans seems like an incredible chore. But if you stop and think for a moment about the great shuddering orgasm that is only a few minutes away, why not go for it?

Can You Really Have an Orgasm with Someone You Have No Chemistry With?

$\mathcal{H}$ere's a seldom talked about subject: having an orgasm with someone you don't even like all that much, someone you don't feel any particular chemistry with. It's not so uncommon. Women do get horny, and sometimes the need to be with a man, almost any man, is so strong, that the woman will just use him. It's not something most women brag about, but it does happen.

You Don't Have to Be Attracted to Your Partner

The physiology of orgasm is such that you don't have to be attracted to someone to get off on them. You can simply use what they've got, like a tool, to get yourself off. Men do it all the time. Do you think men actually have "chemistry" with pornographic images they call up on the Internet, or even the modest pictures potential female partners post of themselves on dating sites? Hell, no! Half the men in America are having sex with women they don't have chemistry with. Some of those women are their wives.

My goddess friend Kendra recalls using a lifeguard at her family's country club to relieve her horny-girl itch. Initially, she found the guy moderately appealing. He didn't actively turn her off. It was a small town. They were both in their early twenties. There weren't many young people that summer hanging around. In retrospect, Kendra thinks they hooked up because they were equally bored and horny.

They were on the dreaded "third date." As everyone knows, the third date is the big one. It's the date when the woman decides whether or not physical intimacy is going to happen. Kendra was disappointed when she realized the lifeguard's kisses weren't giving her the maximum thrill. The problem was that she was already experiencing a sexual tingle. All day long, she had been looking forward to a night of hot sex. She was in the mood, and she needed a partner.

Kendra: *It worked out fine because the guy was so marvelously proficient. I don't know where he learned his techniques or, more likely, what older women taught him some tricks, but he was an able sailor, as they say. He used his fingers to bring me off. It felt so good to come! I knew I needed it, because visiting my family really stresses me out. The orgasm released all that tension for me.*

Real Women Have Real Needs

Real women have needs. Goddesses know how to go about satisfying them. Here's what Vanessa had to say.

Vanessa: *It's not always about the other person. It's about you. It's physical.*

Vanessa says she is not a vibrator person. Humming mechanical equipment is not up her alley. There have been times in her life when she's felt the craving to have a man inside her, when nothing else will substitute. When that happens, she's pragmatic about using what's handy. It's true stories like this that are the basis for all those jokes you ever heard about the horny housewife and the handyman. It's impolitic to say it, but there are horny housewives out there and some of them do jump their handymen! My friend Victor, a landscaper to the rich and famous, has many stories about being beckoned to by the lady of the house for an hour or so of love. It always happened, he said, when he was working near the swimming pool and the lady of the house was on a chaise, sunning. The sun does warm a body up, sometimes to the point of marital indiscretion.

Put Yourself in an Altered State

One way to get over the no-chemistry problem is to put yourself in an altered state. By this I don't necessarily mean a trance, but that is one possibility. More easily induced altered states can be produced by drinking alcohol, smoking pot, or conjuring up an intense mental image.

Jamie readily admits she's had orgasms even when she's with someone she actively dislikes. Not caring about the other person can actually free you up to concentrate completely on your own pleasure.

Jamie: *Oh, you can have an orgasm with someone you might even dislike if you drink enough champagne. Although that might backfire— you can be too drunk to come. There have certainly been times when I've had orgasms with men I barely connected with. I must have liked something about them! Having a vivid imagination helps. You just use that person's body and close your eyes and imagine he is another person. Once I had sex with a guy pretending the whole time he was Brad Pitt.*

Does Using Someone for Your Sexual Purposes Make You a "Slut"?

Some goddesses possess a quality you might call sluttish. Ouch, you say, "slut" is such a harsh word. But real goddesses aren't afraid of it. They know that petty women—and true goddesses are never petty—use the word as a way to mask their jealousy of a woman they think has more sexual charms in her arsenal than she will ever possess. If you plan on becoming a sex goddess, "slut" is a word you need to get over. Insulting a woman who is not afraid to seek out her own pleasure is very ungoddesslike.

Erica likes to fantasize about making love with movie stars when she's feeling less than thrilled with her partner.

Erica: *I have a girlfriend who is bored with having sex with her husband, who she's been with for over thirty years (they met when she was fifteen and have been together since). One night over dinner, she told me the only way she can have an orgasm with him anymore is to pretend she's married to Robert De Niro. I said, "Why him?" I'd have used Hugh Grant, Pierce Brosnan, or that cute elf guy from* Lord of the Rings. *But she's hot for DeNiro. She likes his edginess. Actually, I think her husband is better looking than De Niro, but, hey, it's her fantasy, not mine.*

He's in the Mood. You're Not.

The ability to substitute in your mind one lover for another is an excellent skill for any budding sex goddess. Even if you absolutely adore your partner and enjoy great chemistry, there is going to be at least one day, one time, when your chemistry is off. Consider this situation. You're not in the mood at all, but he or she is. You could claim a headache or cramps and decline to engage in sex at all. There's no rule that says you must have sex when you don't feel like it. Heaven forbid! Every goddess, every woman, has the right of veto power. But there might be times when you don't feel like it, but your partner is really hot for sex. What should you do? As a generous, loving goddess, you can choose to indulge his ardor. In this situation, you have two choices. Will you lie there like a log . . . or are you going to get something for yourself out of it?

Claudia discovered that using a personal lubricant got her in the mood for sex even when something about her partner actually turned her off.

Claudia: *I've surprised myself sometimes. There have been times when I say I don't want to make love with someone and then I do, and it's great and I'm so glad I did it! This happened with one boyfriend. There was a short stretch in our relationship when I just wasn't in the mood for him at all. This is embarrassing to admit, but when I first fell for him, he had a tan. Then he lost it and his pasty white skin was a complete turnoff! Okay, I'm shallow! I didn't have the nerve at the time to tell him that if he didn't hit a tanning salon, our relationship was doomed. He made a move on me after I'd said "no" three times, and I thought, what the heck, and I did just lie there. Like the proverbial log. Well, I don't usually do that, and just the fact it was different triggered something in me. I deliberately didn't move a muscle. I really did play dead. And that made him work harder, like he was bound and determined to arouse me. I started out so dry that he had to use a lubricant. Those things are amazing. They make you wet even when you're not. The harder he worked, and the faster he moved inside me, the more heat and friction he built up. Then my body went on some kind of automatic pilot. My clit swelled up and got hot. I did nothing at all to bring on my orgasm. My body did it all. It just used this guy like a machine. When I came, it was explosive. The very next day, as a present to him and myself, I bought him a package of tanning sessions at the place down the road.*

What's Love Got to Do with It?

If you're in love, or what the psychologists call a "state of limerance," it doesn't take much to make you have an orgasm. You're so turned on and tuned in to the other person that the physical response comes easily. Other times, your orgasm has nothing to do with the other person at all. Instead, it's some particular element of the experience that sends you over the moon. A change of venue, something out of your usual realm, just the fact that the person touching you is someone different, can boost you over the hurdle of No Chemistry.

For Ann, risky situations are particularly arousing.

Ann: *Make it dangerous. Somewhere you might get caught. Outside thrills can get you over the person-to-person thing.*

My goddess friend Chloe says technique trumps chemistry for her every time. She very vividly recalls being extremely hot and bothered over some pretty boys in her youth, only to be disappointed by their clumsy fingers and inefficient tongues, not to mention their youthful jack-rabbit style of intercourse, which, she said, left her high and dry (read "no orgasm") every time. Sometimes if she thought she was madly in love with them that would be enough to get her off. But as an adult woman, she puts a low premium on "love" when it comes to guaranteeing her orgasms.

Chloe: *You can have a great orgasm with someone you don't or can't love. Even chemistry—whatever that really means—has little to do with it. My orgasm is more about the right places being touched and me feeling sexual at the time. I have been in love several times with men who have never given me an orgasm, but have dated men long after their expiration date just because they could send me to orgasm heaven. It's what's in my head and in their fingers, tongues, and abilities to make me feel like the sexy woman I know I am.*

All Orgasms Are Created Equal

There you are, locked in a passionate embrace with your favorite consort or busily engaged in an effervescent, energizing session with your favorite vibrator. From the thin sheen of sweat beading your chest and the way your thigh muscles have gone rigid, orgasm, you know, is imminent. But what kind of orgasm? Will it be a rich, deep clench emanating from the core of your anatomy? Or a succinct electric current localized on your throbbing clitoris? Are you a goddess capable of having different kinds of orgasms? Vive les differences!

Shaking, trembling, slight dizziness, even shortness of breath are all symptoms that under other circumstances would be cause for alarm. They also happen to be the signs of recent orgasm. Many women say they feel drained, even dazed and disoriented for a period of time following their climaxes. Some people claim to be such astute observers of human behavior that they can decipher when a woman has recently had sex—and they're not relying on mussed hair or hastily applied lipstick as the giveaway! A woman who has recently had an orgasm might be flushed, her pupils may be dilated; in the minutes following her climax, she might be a bit off balance, even clumsy. "Knock your socks off" is a good way to describe a memorable orgasm. A deeply situated vaginal orgasm or a rapid-fire series of repeated clitoral ones really can rock your world, if only for a few hours.

Is One Type of Orgasm "Better"?

I think it's a mistake to label one kind of orgasm as "better" than another. It's great if you can experience varying levels of intensity. Ask yourself this: Do you really want to have an orgasm that stops you dead in your tracks every time? It's also a mistake to think you can orchestrate your exact sexual response, even if the stimuli (a vibrator, running water, your own fingers) remains the same. Depending on how tired you are, what your energy level is going into the masturbation/intercourse session, how stressed you are, where you are in your ovulation cycle, and where your hormonal levels are—all of these factors, some of which you have no control over, are going to affect your orgasm, although not in the same way every time. All orgasms are pleasurable; there's no reason to assign value judgments or grade them, unless you're a manic Type-A personality simply hardwired to keep score. Here's what Serena, Helaine, and Vanessa had to say.

Serena: *I very definitely have different types of orgasms. There are the fleeting ones—multiple, consecutive. Then there are the gut-wrenching ones—a big oooooooh! All orgasms are pleasurable, but the more gut-wrenching ones are also more draining. After one, or two, or three (and that's all about I can have), I'm wasted. I'm often shaking for an hour after that.*

Helaine: *I have had orgasms that are so profound and intense that my gums hurt, my scalp lifts. Some are simple and some are short, but others are very long and even have lots of little anal pulses. Those are the best! Afterward, it takes me about ten minutes to remember my name.*

Vanessa: *Orgasms for me used to be totally clitoral-focused, but I've noticed within the past few years (as I've come into my sexual prime),* *the pleasure extends to the surrounding area—inner lips and vagina. I have no reason to believe that there's such a thing as vaginal orgasms. I have not discovered any G-spot, so, like extra terrestrials or God, I have no reason to believe it exists. Everything centers on the clit. When I'm aroused and just my clitoris is being manipulated, there's an overwhelming desire to be penetrated. So even though there's not a vaginal orgasm per se, the parts all work together as one. Get it?*

Vaginal or Clitoral?

The great debate about orgasm always revolves around the question, vaginal or clitoral? I want to make it clear right now that all orgasms are excellent. All orgasms—unless you've been instructed by your physician specifically not to have one—are healthy. Orgasms are life affirming and, from a goddess perspective, that alone makes them worthy.

What's the difference between clitoral and vaginal orgasms? Here are a few basics. Physiologically speaking, a clitoral orgasm is superficial. From an anatomical point of view, the locus of the experience is shallow. The clitoris is located at the very front of the vagina. Women who are very familiar with their clitoris (and if you're going to be a sex goddess, you better be familiar) learn to decipher within their own individual range of response a variety of fine-tuned clitoral sensations. Many women prefer the clitoral orgasm for its sharpness and intensity and because it can be brought on quickly.

Most women are very adept at giving themselves quick clitoral orgasms. Sexually advanced women are aware of their clitoris at all times and have learned to dress, seat themselves, and put their bodies into positions that, if they wish, will constantly stimulate that sweet spot. Any woman can condition her body to be in a low-grade state of arousal 24-7 if she chooses, which is certainly not the worst way to go about the day. Being slightly aroused is certainly an upbeat feeling—possibly the reason some women always seem to have a smile on their faces.

Giulianna: *My orgasms are strongest and most intense when I masturbate, although I do have good orgasms with my partner. All my orgasms originate in the same place, though: my clit. I've had a few experiences with multiple orgasms, but I haven't had one—or is it them?—in years. To be honest, they weren't that special. They were kind of softer than those great shuddering, clenching, screaming orgasms. I like those the best.*

Back in the dark ages—about thirty years ago—clinical sex researchers and many psychotherapists claimed that women who experienced only clitoral orgasms were . . . limited. Women who described their orgasms as clitoral were regarded by these self-described experts (always male) as being immature, juvenile, not fully realized women. Clitoral orgasms, when acknowledged as orgasms at all, were given an inferior status. This kind of widespread denunciation of the clitoral orgasm and its proponents must have left a lot of otherwise healthy, vibrant women depressed. They must have thought there was something wrong with them, because the orgasms they were experiencing—warm, wet, wild, thoroughly enjoyable orgasms—were somehow wrong or insufficient. How sad that makes me feel to think of those women now.

Luckily, thanks mostly to the women's consciousness-raising groups that sprung up in the early '70s, more female physicians, and the advocacy of outspoken sexperts like Dr. Ruth Westheimer, as well as a growing political sense of female empowerment, the clitoral orgasm is now regarded as a dynamic and separate orgasmic entity unto itself. The clitoral orgasm is usually produced by direct stimulation of the clitoris. That stimulation might come from masturbation or from a partner's finger or tongue. Less commonly, it can also be brought on by indirect stimulation by the penis as it moves in and out of the vagina during intercourse.

Women who are able to achieve a clitoral orgasm during regular intercourse have figured out the best way for them to position their bodies while making love. This can be achieved by elevating the hips, or placing a pillow beneath one's posterior, or by the woman raising her legs high in the air, or scissoring her legs while she is being penetrated. Sometimes positioning the woman's legs to hang over her partner's shoulders works. All of these positions bring the clitoris into direct contact with the penis during the act of love.

Psychotherapists (put Sigmund Freud at the top of the list) who decried the vaginal orgasm as juvenile had their own interests to protect, since clitoral orgasm often has little to do with the male member. In the days when premarital sex was severely frowned on, "nice" people chose to take the position that only happily married women, those who were engaging in socially sanctified sex, could achieve orgasm. Family doctors routinely told women right up until the 1970s that if they weren't having vaginal orgasms, they weren't having a legitimate orgasm, which some-how reflected on their husbands. Not only was it your marital duty to have sex, but you had to have a vaginal orgasm as well.

Stimulating the Clitoris with Fingers or Thrusts

Is it possible to have a clitoral orgasm during traditional inter-course even if you haven't yet come upon your optimal sexual position? Yes. Here's where your partner's experience or willing-ness to experiment makes a difference. A man who is genuinely interested in pleasing his partner learns to caress the clitoris with his thumb while he is inside his lover, or takes the time to arouse his partner's clitoris sufficiently with either tongue or fingers before penetration, so that the indirect pressure the clitoris receives as the penis does its thrusting is sufficient to produce a clitoral orgasm. The clitoris can be stimulated with fingers or a tongue after the man has had his climax. If the relationship is an established one and the partners are expert at producing pleasure within and for each other, the man may slow down his thrusts and draw them out in a way that his partner can experience a series of small clitoral orgasms or wavelets throughout the sex act from indirect clitoral/penile contact. Women who regularly pleasure themselves with dildos and enjoy the deep penetration they can have with them learn how to give themselves clitoral orgasms this way as well.

Here's what a few of the correspondents had to say on the subject.

Jamie: *For me, there are definite differences between a clitoral orgasm and a vaginal one. They're both pleasurable, although they do vary in intensity. My vibrator gives me the most intense clitoral orgasms, which truthfully can sometimes ride the fence between pleasure and pain. If I use it for too long or at too high a setting, the sensation can be almost numbing, even if for a while it feels good.*

Samantha: *I would describe my orgasms as clitoral. They vary in feeling from a pleasurable tickle to a moderate throbbing. I would describe them generally as small electrical shocks—but in a good way—that can occur in either waves or small bursts that repeat themselves if my partner hones in on exactly the right spot and keeps going.*

Some Women's Vaginal Orgasms Are "More Profound"

If clitoral orgasms, enjoyable as they are, can be described as "superficial," women who have vaginal orgasms often call theirs "profound." What is a vaginal orgasm, anyway? Some goddesses describe the feeling as a kind of slow-building internal earthquake. Others say their vaginal orgasms make the earth move or time stand still, depending on their preferred metaphor. Although many women who greatly enjoy sex say they have never experienced a vaginal orgasm, it can and does exist. Possibly the original sex researchers such as Kinsey were right in calling it the orgasm of the mature woman, because young girls and even very sexually active women in their twenties and thirties often never have the experience and don't know what they are missing.

The vaginal orgasm *is* profound. It happens deep inside the body, the vibrations affecting not only the vaginal passage, but the uterus itself. The vaginal orgasm is slow to build. Usually, after a protracted period of foreplay and several clitoral orgasms, a momentum builds until the entire reproductive system is vibrating, culminating in an explosive burst. It used to be that the only way to achieve a vaginal orgasm was with a partner whose penis was long enough to repeatedly knock on the door of the womb, although now some sex toy stores sell an object known as a G-spot finder that is said to do the trick. I don't want to make too much of the vaginal orgasm, since not every woman has them, and they are certainly not necessary to enjoying a fulfilling sex life. Some women never have a vaginal orgasm and are still very secure, sexually satisfied people. But once you've had one, you know it. Some goddesses say they believe the vaginal orgasm is the best orgasm of all. Others say it's just another orgasm to enjoy and experience in their overall repertoire. Jamie loves her vaginal orgasms, but she finds them exhausting.

Jamie: *My vaginal orgasms, while requiring a clitoral element to set them off, are much deeper, more complex, far more intense. For me, there is nothing better or closer than being penetrated and to experience that fullness of having a man inside me and the completeness that brings. I enjoy the feeling of having a penis inside me and the thrusting that goes along with it. While it takes more "whole body" physical action to make the vaginal orgasm happen, when it does, it is very overwhelming and also very exhausting.*

Today, most women know that they can have more than one kind of orgasm—two kinds at least. Actually, there are several different orgasms any woman can experience. In fact, there is an entire spectrum of orgasms ranging from the tiniest ripples to true mind-blowers. Here is how I describe them.

The Tickle Orgasm

There is really no other way to describe the tickle orgasm. It is just a tickle, but what an exciting tickle it is. You may experience the tickle orgasm when your eye falls on someone who is an Instant Love Object, someone so beautiful, so sexy, so appealing, someone you so want to grab right now that your clitoris becomes instantly electrified. The reaction to this stimulus might be that you feel you need to immediately masturbate to bring yourself release. But sometimes you can have a tickle orgasm without even touching yourself. Personally, I have experienced these tickle orgasms on many occasions by merely rubbing the tops of my thighs together if I happen to be sitting down, or by doing an internal rolling motion that pushes my labia together. Practice clenching your labia together. After you've learned how to clench, next practice flexing them. You may feel this exercise is similar to learning how to wiggle your ears, but it's definitely worth doing. The tickle orgasm is over so fast that it can seem like it never happened. Except you know it did, and now you can't get out of your mind how much you want it to happen again.

The Multiphasic Orgasm

The multiphasic orgasm can last from moments to minutes, depending on the stimuli and the time frame the goddess who is having it can devote to continuing it. The multiphasic orgasm can be honed and self-taught through long practice sessions at masturbation. If you are willing to devote time to this art and practice, you will be able to achieve expert status as a multiphasic orgasm-er in no time at all.

The multiphasic orgasm is all about peaks and valleys. Actually, it's a bit more spread out than that—think mountains and medium hilltops and rolling meadows and some riverbeds and everything in between. Or if geographic references are not your cup of tea, think of the multiphasic orgasm in terms of opera and arias—high notes, low notes, medium notes. As long as the music keeps flowing, it's all fabulous.

Multiphasic orgasms tend to go on and on. Women who have not achieved or are not yet aware of their sex goddess status sometimes don't discern the differences between multiphasic orgasms and another kind of orgasm I call Simple Multiple Orgasm, or SMO. This is a series of orgasms that arrive at the same level of intensity and come in a rapid-fire or marginally spaced-out sequence. SMOs arrive either staccato-like, one right after the other, or they may arrive with fifteen-minute rests in between, which can happen if you are making love with a partner for hours. The multiphasic orgasm is not like that. It's more like one big, long orgasm that has a great deal of sighing and breathing in between. Sighing, like breathing, by the way, is a tension releaser. An advanced yoga practitioner, Ava, has this to say about the subject.

My own yoga and sexual experiences have taught me that the most important thing is to keep breathing. The flow of your orgasmic experience should not be interrupted. Deep, full body breathing will facilitate and accentuate your orgasm(s). Holding your breath causes tension and may even cut off the flow of orgasm and orgasmic sensations. The breath is a mirror of your emotions and your physical state. As you become excited, your breathing may speed up and reflect your level of arousal. Let your breath stay connected to your body sensation, and everything will follow its natural course.

The Simple Multiple Orgasm

You're coming and coming and coming. The flow might be constant—you have two, three, even four orgasms right in a row with barely a breath in between. Or you've been masturbating with your vibrator or making love for hours with your partner all afternoon or late into the night, experiencing orgasm after orgasm with ten- or fifteen-minute breaks in between. If your partner has taken Viagra and the lovemaking is without end, you are a good candidate for experiencing SMO orgasms. Couples who practice Tantric yoga together very often schedule orchestrated lovemaking sessions whose very purpose is to elicit SMO orgasms. These orgasms, unlike multiphasic ones, tend to fit on the same Richter scale, as it were, of orgasmic calibration. If the first one rates a five for example, all of them will rate about a five, as well. Women who are capable of experiencing SMO orgasms are often talented self-pleasurers who have, over time, conditioned their bodies to respond well to specific stimuli. SMO orgasms are almost always clitoral. Many women experience them from a long, languorous session of oral sex, when the person doing the licking avoids much contact with the clitoris (it becomes too sensitive and can be actually painful), concentrating instead on a lavish licking and sucking and kissing of the labia and the area directly to the right or the left of the clitoris instead. Other women say they can experience these multiple orgasms from standard intercourse if they have been sufficiently aroused with a long session of foreplay before penetration begins.

The Energy Orgasm

Believe it or not, there are some goddesses so advanced at using their own energy—the electromagnetic impulses surging inside us—as the stimulating agent, that they don't need anything else beyond a Lust Object to focus on. These goddesses are very special.

Through their many sexual escapades and years of experimentation (usually these goddesses are champion masturbators, too), these lucky deities can experience orgasm—most often tingly, clitoral ones—simply by putting themselves in close proximity to another person. They use their energy (or vibration, if you like) in conjunction with the other person's to stoke an erotic fire resulting in instantaneous orgasm. The truly remarkable thing about an energy orgasm is that the lust object need not even be an active participant. They may be only dimly aware of their role as the fire starter. Often they are an unwitting contributor to the orgasm that the goddess seated or standing next to them is having. I have had the amazing fortune to have experienced the energy orgasm myself. It is mind-blowing. The orgasm produced is bright, intense, and ephemeral. It has come upon me so fast that if I didn't know my own body so well, I'd think I was caught up in a waking dream or hallucination. That's another marvelous thing about the energy orgasm. It's the closest thing you'll ever get to tripping in public, in broad daylight, even in a coffee bar—and you don't need to take Ecstasy to experience it.

Here's what a few of the correspondents had to say about their different types of orgasms.

Samantha: *I'm often surprised at the different paths my orgasms will take. Sometimes I'll be highly aroused from foreplay and I'll feel like I might climax any second, only to reach that point and find my body is backing down and won't go there. Other times, I might not feel so obviously aroused, and yet I'll have an orgasm sneak up on me anyway! I don't disagree that you can pretty much determine what kind of orgasm you're going to have. It's just that it's still mysterious to me how my mind and body work together to make one of them happen.*

Serena: *My clitoral and vaginal orgasms are decidedly different. Both are pleasurable, but they are distinctly not the same!*

Taryn: *When pleasuring myself, I don't have the pressure of having to "hurry up" or match my partner or feel that sense of performing in bed. Those are always clitoral orgasms, and sometimes I can have a few of them, fast, in a row. I can only have an orgasm from receiving oral sex if I'm really relaxed, which isn't often. If I'm a little bit stressed, I often can't have an orgasm. If I'm really stressed, I don't want to have sex. Maybe that's why I enjoy early morning sex. I'm not awake enough to know if I'm stressed.*

Helaine: *Give me a vaginal orgasm over the clitoral one. It's more satisfying to me.*

Carole: *I can't tell the difference between a clitoral or a vaginal orgasm. They both feel the same, or maybe I'm just having both kinds simultaneously.*

Erica: *I'm not sure I know the difference between a clitoral or a vaginal orgasm. It all just feels good to me.*

Finding Your G-Spot

*T*he G-spot orgasm phenomena began in earnest in 1983 when the writers and sex researchers Alice Kahn Ladas, Beverly Whipple, and John D. Perry published their seminal work, *The G-Spot and Other Recent Discoveries About Human Sexuality*. Their book spent two months on best-seller lists and became one of the most talked about books in years. It was eaten up, almost literally, by American women, who were captivated by the idea that there was a new sexual experience out there they hadn't yet sampled. *The San Francisco Chronicle* called the book "damn convincing," and *Time* magazine heralded it for championing the existence of a bean-shaped erogenous zone no one had ever seen, let alone talked about, supposedly located deep within the female vagina.

Despite the number of words written about the G-spot (at one time or another it seems every women's magazine in America has had an article on it), there is still a lot of confusion about what a G-spot orgasm is or where a woman can find her own G-spot.

Shane: *I think the G-spot is a myth. It's like the Holy Grail. I wish I could find mine. I've been hearing about the G-spot for years, reading about it in magazines, but I can't say I've ever experienced anything that I would call a G-spot orgasm in my life. And it's not like I haven't been having sex for a long time. At this point, I'm not even sure that I would know it if I had a G-spot orgasm, but I'd love to have the chance to find out! If only I could find a partner who would help me find my G-spot and give me one of those G-spot orgasms, I think I'd be catapulted into seventh heaven.*

Erica: *I don't know what a G-spot orgasm is.*

Suzette: *What the hell is a G-spot orgasm anyway? What is it? Everything I read about it makes it sound like something I'm having anyway.*

When stimulated, the G-spot is believed to produce a kind of orgasm that is distinctly different from other orgasms women describe having. After Ladas, Whipple, and Perry's book was published, it wasn't long before media wranglers jumped on the bandwagon predicting the discovery of this hitherto unknown portion of the female anatomy would liberate women said to be suffering from sexual dysfunction. Sex therapists began encouraging their clients to stimulate their G-spots. The revelations given in the book from women of all ages and all walks of life who had experienced the G-spot orgasm helped alleviate the anxiety of many women who thought the fluid they emitted after their orgasms was urine. Women who were embarrassed or felt ashamed of their own body fluids and who believed they had been peeing in bed were now told that the liquid flowing out of them was female ejaculation. Unfortunately for generations of women, the information came too late. They may have had partners who belittled them because they thought they were urinating. As a consequence, many older women had learned to suppress their orgasms because of these negative experiences; what should have been so thrilling turned out to be, for them, humiliating.

Hopefully, those dark days of shame are over.

Samantha: *I think I had a G-spot orgasm once, but I can't be sure. I had a partner who was very gifted with his hands and who gave me an orgasm through simultaneous clitoral and internal stimulation with his fingers. It was a very different orgasm than anything I'd previously experienced, so there might have been some G-spot thing going on.*

Here are some facts you should know about the G-spot.

- The G-spot is named for Ernst Grafenberg, a German gynecologist.
- The G-spot is a bean-shaped patch of erectile tissue located in the front wall of the vagina, directly behind the pubic bone.
- Some medical doctors and sex researchers have tried to make the case that the organ acts as a second clitoris.
- The spot itself is composed of a network of blood vessels, glands and ducts, nerve endings, and the surrounding tissue at the neck of the bladder.
- Women who have experienced the G-spot orgasm never forget it.

Taryn: *One of the best orgasms I ever had was in a car during intercourse, missionary position, in the front seat with the seat reclined. It was after much oral sex and a lot of foreplay. The person had an unusually large penis, and I believe he was able to hit my G-spot in just the right way to produce an incredible orgasm!*

The G-spot is extremely sensitive to pressure. It lies in the anterior wall of the vagina about two inches from the entrance. When stimulated, either by fingers or a penis, the spot swells and leads to orgasm in a majority of women. The sex researchers Whipple and Perry noted that many women appeared to ejaculate a liquid through the urethra (which is also where urine is expelled) that is chemically similar to male ejaculate, albeit with no sperm.

Some Positions Work Better Than Others

The G-spot is more difficult to reach through intercourse in the missionary position. Other positions work better. Some women say that when their partners penetrate them shallowly (as opposed to deep penetration), they are more likely to have the penis hit the G-spot. Some women report that the use of the diaphragm for birth control interferes with hitting the G-spot.

You Might Not Always Have a G-Spot Orgasm

The G-spot orgasm is special. Even women like Carole and Chelsea who are used to having regular orgasms say they don't have a G-spot orgasm all the time.

Carole: *I had a G-spot orgasm once. I can't remember any of the details, but I do remember hubby hitting the spot. Once!*

Chelsea: *In my whole life, I've had two G-spot orgasms. I wasn't really sure what was happening at the time. It was so pleasurable, but it didn't feel like my normal clitoral orgasms. Afterwards, I had a gush of fluid. At the time, I was embarrassed. I thought I had peed, but it didn't smell anything like urine.*

Today every woman wants to know more about her G-spot. If you're looking for yours, try this: The spot is located directly behind the pubic bone within the front wall of your vagina. It's about halfway between the back of your pubic bone and the front of the cervix. You won't be able to see it even if you're crouching on the floor of your bathroom squatting over a mirror. (This is a good way, however, to minutely study your labia and clitoris.) But you don't need to see your G-spot to prove its existence.

More on Finding Yours

To find your G-spot, don't bother lying on your back. Gravity works against you because it pulls the organs down. Unless you have exceptionally long fingers and are not squeamish about pushing them far inside you, this is not the best way to find your own sweet spot. A sitting or squatting position works much better. Sitting on the toilet is good. From this position, you can explore the upper front wall of your vagina by pushing firmly upward with your fingers inside your body. When you find it, it will feel like a small bean. You'll find it faster if you simultaneously apply a downward pressure with your other hand outside your body just above the pubic bone.

As you stimulate the G-spot by applying pressure on it, the spot will begin to swell. You may experience it as a small lump between your fingers. You will feel a distinct internal sensation that will stop the moment you let up on the pressure.

Your first impression when you touch the spot might feel like you're going to urinate. If you're on a G-spot search mission, relieve yourself first. Next, stroke the area where you "feel the bean" with a firm but gentle touch. At this point, you may feel a quick contraction in your uterus.

Take the time to play and experiment with different levels of touching your G-spot the way you have played with and experimented with different touches on your clitoris. Most women say they can put a lot more pressure on their G-spot than they can handle on their clitoris. The clitoris is a far more delicate and sensitive organ, for sure. After you have learned how you like your G-spot touched, your next step is to teach your partner, to guide him to do the exact same search method you just did to yourself. It'll take patience and time and may not even feel particularly erotic the first time you're telling him how to find it. It's a little like getting him to play gynecologist. Once he knows where it is, the two of you can incorporate his massaging it into your foreplay and hopefully let your orgasms begin.

Step-by-Step Tips to Help Your Partner
Find Your G-spot

- When working with a partner, try lying facedown on a bed. Your legs should be apart and your butt should be a bit elevated.

- Ask your partner to insert two fingers (palm down) into your vagina. Ask him to carefully explore the front wall of your vagina, which is the part that is closest to the bed. He should use a firm but gentle touch.

- At this point, you can wriggle your hips a bit to help him find the spot. Communication with your partner at this point is essential. Don't make him grope blindly in the dark.

- To help your partner locate your G-spot, recline on your back. Your partner should insert one or two fingers (palm up) into your vagina.

- The spot can usually be found when your partner puts pressure against the top wall of the vagina, about halfway between the back of the pubic bone and the end of the vagina where the cervix is.

- Either you or your partner can put a second hand on top of the abdomen just above the pubic hairline and gently push down.

Best Position with a Partner
for Finding Your G-Spot

The female superior position is a good one for locating and stimulating the G-spot. The advantage is that you or your partner can apply extra pressure above your pubic bone from the outside of

your body. The woman on top—or what I call Goddess Superior—
position also allows you the freedom to move around and to keep
repositioning yourself until your partner's penis hits just the right
spot. The angle of your partner's penis also has a lot to do with
whether or not he can hit it. A penis that points straight up is
more versatile than one that tilts like the Leaning Tower of Pisa
in either an easterly or westerly direction.

Other Positions for Finding Your G-Spot

Of course, the G-spot can be stimulated from intercourse in the
missionary position. However, it takes a very particular penis that
configures perfectly with the interior of that woman's body. Some
women say a large penis finds the spot better, while others say a
shorter, thicker penis works best for them. Possibly there is no one
right kind of penis, because each woman's vagina is slightly different, just as every man's penis is.

Take the time to experiment with locating and touching your
G-spot. The orgasms it produces are both intense and profound.
Some women have described it as earthshaking. You might not
need to have that kind of orgasm every time. It might be something you save for occasions when you and your partner have a
few hours devoted to making love. It's definitely not for quickie
sex, unless your partner knows your body very well and is very
well versed in all the ways he or she can please it.

Finding Your G-Spot with a Sex Toy
or Masturbation Tool

You can use a vibrator or dildo to stimulate your G-spot. A woman
masturbating can fondle her vulva and stimulate her clitoris if she
chooses with one hand (or her vibrator) while using her free hand

to press down on her own abdomen just above the pubic bone. Chloe reported her recent discovery of a sex toy called a G-Spot Finder.

Chloe: *I bought mine from a London store. It is made of a Lucite-type material. I tried it and nothing happened. I think I am having a hard time finding this spot. I thought I was buying something that would vibrate the G-spot, but I have now looked at several of these things and they all are just solid lumps. They look like a penis with a little hard min-iature penis attached to the side. The main part goes in you and the little part supposedly hits the spot. But so far, it hasn't!*

I apprised Chloe that her new G-spot vibrator would work fine, but there is a trick to using it. For starters, it can't be the first tool you pull out of your box. A G-spot orgasm is difficult to have unless you've had a clitoral orgasm first or at least you've been hanging on a plateau of high arousal for some time. The G-spot orgasm is best achieved not as the first orgasm of the session, but something to be worked up to after you've been well-primed for love.

Shopping for Your Own G-Spot Stimulator

The problem with buying sex tools and toys is that the G-spot stimulators, vibrators, and dildos advertised all look about the same. The G-spot stimulators look like regular dildos and vibrators except they are curved. Supposedly the bend is the part that hits the G-spot. There are many G-spot stimulators advertised, but it's a case of buyer beware. Until a woman designs the right piece of equipment, chances are none of what's currently available is ever going to work. If you can find a dildo or vibrator with a curved piece at the top, that's your best bet, although be prepared to root around for a while before you discover your own sweet spot.

Female Ejaculation—Fact or Fantasy?

The historical literature on the subject is scanty. Physicians who have known about it for the most part have kept their knowledge to themselves. A Victorian era novel called *The Pearl* describes ejaculating females, but the work has long been dismissed as pornography. As far back as 1926, a medical doctor, Theodore Van de Velde, published a popular marriage manual called *Ideal Marriage*, in which he described female ejaculation. Physical and cultural anthropologists have noted that the Batoro tribe of Uganda actually has a custom that revolves around female ejaculation called "kachapati," which means to spatter the wall. The gynecologist and sexual researcher Ernst Grafenberg, Dr. G-spot himself, wrote a detailed description of female ejaculation that commented on fluid released at the moment of orgasm. In his description, he used the word "gushes." In 1966, the sex researchers Masters and Johnson called female ejaculation "an erroneous concept," although some years earlier the sex researcher Albert Kinsey gave the topic a bit more attention. In her book *The Female Eunuch*, published in 1970, Germaine Greer talked about how many men refuted the idea of a female ejaculation and seemed herself to deem it impossible.

Yet many women report waking up with "wet dreams" just as men do, their sheets puddled with a fluid that does not resemble urine. If it's not, what is it? A quick search on the Web offers dozens of entries posted on medical sites. In 1990, a physician, H. Alzate, published his opinions on vaginal erogeneity, the G-spot, and female ejaculation in the *Journal of Sex Education and Therapy*. Dr. Beverly Whipple wrote more about female ejaculation in 2000 in the *Journal of Sex Research*. Dr. Susan Block, a sex therapist, calls female ejaculation "one of the great sexual wonders of the world" in her online journal, which can be found at www.drsusanblock.com. Twenty-five years ago, female ejaculation was documented in the world of adult movies, as a young woman named Fallon, a pornographic actress, apparently produced an ejaculate during her on-screen orgasms. She became known as "Fallon, the Squirting Girl." It was hotly debated among porn movie reviewers whether or not the liquid spurting out of Fallon's body was urine, something artificially produced for the films, or the young woman's natural secretions. Those who say female ejaculate is real agree on two points. They say the liquid that is ejaculated is not the color of urine and it does not smell or taste like it, either. The taste, in fact, has been described as both tangy and sweet.

Female ejaculation is rare. It is believed that only about ten percent of women can do it, and many of those women have "trained" themselves not to, for fear that they will be called bed wetters. But female ejaculation is a very special gift.

Correspondents' Experiences with Female Ejaculation

Serena had a special name for it.

Serena: *Yes, I've had it, but only when I've been terrifically aroused. I call that zone the "deep purple."*

Samantha wasn't sure if what she experienced was female ejaculation or not.

Samantha: *I tend to get very wet when I'm aroused, so it's hard for me to say if I experience a "big gush" or not. I have, on occasion, been stimulated to the point where I feel additional fluids flowing, but wondered if it was urine from having a full or semi-full bladder at the time of sex. But there have been occasions when I know my bladder is empty when this sensation has occurred, so I guess I have a female ejaculation.*

Suzette experienced something, but she wouldn't call it a "gush."

Suzette: *It feels like I've had a big gush, but in reality I think it's more of a piddling trickle.*

Taryn had the experience, but she didn't exactly love it.

Taryn: *I've had a female ejaculation, and I must say: what a mess!*

For Chelsea, the main thing she felt was a sort of pleased embarrassment.

Chelsea: *It was quite embarrassing for me. I thought it was urine. I think my partner thought it was urine, too. It's happened a few times and now I'm not so embarrassed, but it is a little bit annoying because it means I have to get up right away and change the sheets.*

Kendra prepares for the gush by positioning towels on the bed.

Kendra: *I have absolutely had a female ejaculation. With certain partners, I know in advance I need to put a towel doubled up under myself on the bed. It doesn't happen every time, but if I haven't had an orgasm in a while, I think that stuff builds up.*

Here's what some of the men had to say:

Peter thinks of finding a woman who can ejaculate as something wonderful to look forward to.

Peter: *I've never witnessed what I thought was a female ejaculation. I've never had a woman say, "Watch this, I'm going to come." It is something to look forward to, I guess!*

Ray described the experience as being "unique."

Ray: *One woman did ejaculate from finger stimulation I gave her when we were reclining together on a couch. I saw it! I was amazed! I consider it unique. I saw it flowing out. It was amazing. Too bad the relationship wasn't working out otherwise.*

Keith felt like he was witnessing a miracle.

Keith: *I saw it, it happened, it happened multiple times! The first time I was in high school. She was on top and when she had her orgasm (and a very loud, vocal orgasm it was, too), I felt a gush of liquid. At that age, I was so inexperienced I thought I'd broken something—popped it! Another time, with another woman, she was also on top. At one point, her face went completely blank and then suddenly contorted. I watched, she came. The gush was warm and very plentiful. I touched it, sniffed it. It was a pale, clear, sweet-smelling liquid. With yet another woman, I found her sweet spot and worked on it, and she had numerous gushes. I kid you not, it went on for several moments. I stayed with this woman for a long time and she was the master—make that mistress—of female ejaculation. One time she gushed so hard it splashed up in my face. I was soaked, but I felt great. Did I like it? Hell. I've been searching for another gushing gal ever since!*

PART VI

The Zen of Goddess Orgasm

The point of living should be to experience bliss.
—Goddess motto

Breathe Deep

𝔍 once watched an extraordinary tape called *Ancient Secrets of Sexual Ecstasy for Modern Lovers*, produced by Higher Love Video Series at Tantra.com. I am sure you can find it on the Internet. The tape was given to me by a goddess friend who is deeply into yoga. It is a strange tape. It might even freak you out. This is not your ordinary how-to-have-better-sex video. It is an instructional guide, but it was shot either back in the sex-mad 1970s (and what a hedonistic epoch that was in the annals of human sexuality!) or the couples who shared their love and lovemaking techniques made the video as a message to lovers everywhere. Their appearance is so different from what our culture has come to expect when watching human beings interact so intimately on tape or film. In our age of cruelty and contempt for those who have not been gifted with beauty and physical perfection or lack the means to buy it, these lovers are not terribly appealing. In other words, they don't resemble gods and goddesses. They have pleasant, if unfashionable, bodies. One of the women has a post-childbirth belly that sags. The men have hair on their backs. Everybody has hair under their arms. The women have bushes. Yes. Bushes. Real, untrimmed, pubic bushes! The hair factor alone makes the tape both fearful and fascinating. But though they are mere mortals—like ordinary people you see every day, albeit clothed—when they climb the mountain of Eros together, they are transformed into gods and goddesses.

Tantric Breathing Techniques

But it's not the man-to-woman sex that makes *Ancient Secrets of Sexual Ecstasy for Modern Lovers* so amazing. About three-quarters of the way through the tape, a woman comes on the screen and talks a little bit about Tantric breathing techniques that a woman can learn to do to bring herself to orgasm. This is the part my friend meant me to watch. She said she had not seen the tape herself, but that she had witnessed a yoga teacher perform this breathing orgasm stunt at a yoga retreat she had attended. I was skeptical when she told me about the tape. Until I saw it for myself, I didn't have enough faith in the power of breathing. Then I watched two different women utilizing breathing techniques to bring themselves to shattering orgasms without even touching themselves.

The average human orgasm lasts twelve seconds. Pigs, by the way, have orgasms lasting up to thirty minutes. Instead of wasting your time or energy on envy, try some ancient Tantric breathing techniques instead. You can extend those tantalizingly brief seconds of bliss for much longer. Much, much longer!

Changing Your Orgasms Forever

How much bliss you can handle is really up to you. By learning yoga pranayama breathing techniques, a woman can change her orgasms forever. Pranayama, which in yoga parlance means "breath control," is the the fourth limb of yoga. Pranayama is a series of specific breathing exercises where the breath is regulated and controlled by the length or duration of each inhalation and the length or duration of each exhalation. The pauses, or retention, between each breath are important, too. In Sanskrit, "prana" is the cosmic energy manifest in the breath. In Sanskrit, the word "ayama" means "expansion" or "to increase." *The Everything Yoga Book*, by Cynthia Worby, describes pranayama as the process in which the prana is developed and strengthened in the body to purify the nervous system and to increase a person's vital life energy. Pranayama breathing leading to orgasm is a little-known element of yoga, not even well understood by established yoga teachers. Its techniques have been practiced for centuries by yoga enthusiasts in remote ashrams, the knowledge and history passed down through the generations in practice and in handwritten books.

As Simple as Inhaling and Exhaling

Pranayama breathing is as simple as inhaling and exhaling. The inhale sets you back, the exhale pushes you forward. The breathing is done while you lie on your back. In *Ancient Secrets of Sexual Ecstasy for Modern Lovers*, two women separately perform the breathing routines. Each starts in a position where their knees are raised to their chests. The hands remain at the sides. They each pushed their torsos toward the ceiling using their hands and the balls of their feet for leverage. Using what yogis call "Fire Breath," they visualized their sexual energy moving up their bodies until they were spontaneously undulating their spines. Next, using "Ecstasy Breath," which is a more generalized vibration, they let their jaws fall open and engaged in long, slow, deep breaths.

It took about eight minutes for the first woman to bring herself to a peak level of arousal. She experienced a long, deep orgasm that I recognized as vaginal. Her entire pelvis was undulating as she rode the wave of what appeared to be repeated contractions as deep and primordial as the contractions of advanced childbirth, until she was caught up in a spasm of pleasure. The other woman began the same way, but used her breath to bring herself right to the peak of her climax. Instead of going forward and finishing the climax, she stayed poised right on the crest. Using only her breath, not her hands at all, she inhaled and exhaled herself over and over to peak arousal, then, using different breaths, brought herself up and down. This is the way it went, up and down, over and over and over, until her body was vibrating in full orgasmic splendor.

It can be embarrassing to some women to have their partners see how they look when they come. The face is often contorted, you may be breathless and flushed, you might feel you look silly or too exposed or even ugly. It is the fear of being so nakedly exposed that keeps some women from fully letting go and giving themselves over to their full orgasmic pleasure. Be aware that no matter how funny you think you look when you are in this exalted state of bliss, your partner will find you extraordinarily beautiful at this moment.

The Zen of Goddess Orgasm

J asked my goddess friends to describe what they most enjoy about their orgasms. Is it simply the physical release? Or do they attach or attribute any meaning beyond physical sensation to the experience? Here's what they said.

Samantha most loves the orgasms she shares with a partner.

Samantha: *I love the intensity, the euphoria, the feeling of release I get from my orgasms that I share with a partner. I tend not to feel as deeply about achieving orgasm alone. At best, it's just done for the quick physical release and I wind up feeling like a "cheap date." Being alone and having an orgasm can't compare for me to being with a partner. As I'm not prone to having casual sex, most of the sexual experiences I have are with men I'm fond of and close to, and in the best cases somewhat in love with or feel a strong emotional connection to. In the cases of those I'm feeling passionately in love with, the orgasm feels that much more acute and almost spiritual. That comes as a direct result of the clichéd feeling of "oneness" that occurs with someone during the act and release, particularly if the orgasm comes from intercourse. The best lover I ever had was someone I was intensely in love with and with whom I had an amazing, karmically sexual connection. Having sex and orgasm with this particular person was truly nirvana. I felt as if my entire soul floated out of my body in the process, and that it lingered over us. The absolute best experience I ever had—if only I could connect this way again with someone new.*

Jolie feels her orgasms feed her soul.

Jolie: *I love having orgasms. They feed the soul and spirit, as well as stimulate the body. I think they're part of what makes us human. It's this humanity and the emotional quotient that really elevate all of the sexual experience—the pleasure, the climax, the acts of giving and receiving. For me, what's so great about sex is that it disengages my brain. The climax is a great release, rejuvenating me and, if I'm having sex with a partner, often strengthening and renewing the relationship.*

Serena is in awe of the power she personally experiences from having orgasms.

Serena: *Orgasm is powerful. I think we direct it, so it is one way we give ourselves control over our lives. Plus, it's such a release—better than a therapist, drugs or drink (Ok, maybe not wine). Orgasm helps me relax, sleep, concentrate. Most importantly, I think it helps me feel smart, beautiful, and sexual. After all, isn't this what all spiritual women desire?*

For Taryn, there is a clearly spiritual element.

Taryn: *I don't know if this is what people mean when they say something is spiritual, but orgasm does make me feel more connected to my partner.*

Carole loves the feeling of peace she gets from her orgasms.

Carole: *What I love about my orgasms is the feeling I get from them of peace, calm, and satisfaction.*

Roxanne loves the feeling of closeness she can share with her partner.

Roxanne: *I love feeling totally close to my partner. This is why I don't want to have an orgasm with just anyone. I want that intimacy to be reciprocal and long lasting. For me, orgasms are totally spiritual. The* *spirituality is a core component. I also love that I am totally unable to think about anything else when one is happening, which also, by the way, makes me feel extremely exposed and vulnerable.*

Erica relishes the connection she feels sharing her orgasm with someone she loves.

Erica: *Having an orgasm with my partner brings us together in a more connected way. It allows us to feel more together, rather than just being together. It also brings us joy, knowing that we can please each other.*

Kendra hopes her orgasms will keep her forever young.

Kendra: *I enjoy the rocket-ship aspect of orgasm. The way it projects you waaaay out into the atmosphere. I think that is so healthy. I'm convinced that lack of orgasms is directly related to aging. So I've got to go out and get me more—soon!*

It's the high Suzette is always going for.

Suzette: *I enjoy the high. Is orgasm a spiritual experience for me? Hard to say, but it definitely is an out-of-body experience.*

Giulianna loves the idea of a natural gift of pure pleasure.

Giulianna: *Having an orgasm makes me feel satisfied, content, comforted. I find that whether I am alone or with a partner, orgasm is a way for me to feel more connected to either a partner or myself. It cleanses me of pent-up energy and stress. There have been some wonderful and adept partners I was never able to have an orgasm with, and I still wonder why. Why didn't I trust myself enough to let go? Which brings me to the point that orgasm also makes me feel vulnerable, as exposed as I possibly could be. Once the boundary is crossed, I feel a great sense of accomplishment. It's not like that for men, whose orgasms seem* *almost involuntary And it's not a mere physical catharsis either, like a sneeze. Since a woman doesn't need to have an orgasm to make a baby—and a man does—my conclusion is that her orgasm is special because it is the feminine gift of pure pleasure.*

Possibly Chelsea says it best.

Chelsea: *This might sound clichéd, but my favorite part of orgasm is the point where that's the only thought in my head, like I would do anything to make this feeling continue and that I'm completely connected to my partner and he is giving me more pleasure almost than I can stand without losing everything completely. I feel in control because I'm making this happen, yet powerless also because my desire for this is overwhelming. It's a balance between those two emotions, but neither is diluted. My movements, along with his touching me in order to please me, are making this thing happen, so I prefer the assertive posture. But I'm also so totally engaged in the experience that I can barely breathe and I don't care what I look like. I don't care if others might be watching. All I can think about is that sweet point where it all releases and contracts and consumes all rational thought. That's what I'm always going for.*

Feminine Orgasm: A Male Point of View

This was a chance for the fellas to put in their two cents. I asked them if they had one piece of advice to share with women about how to make their partner's orgasms better or how to have them more often, what would that advice be? Here's what they said.

Curt: *Relax and don't concentrate on having an orgasm. Focus on what is happening in your body and enjoy whatever sensations arise.*

Keith: *Drop the emotional baggage and consider your partner and his member to be there for your exclusive pleasure-filled use. Don't worry about him. He'll spurt at the drop of a hat. The bottom line is go get* *yours! Do whatever is necessary. Close your eyes and pretend he's the stud gardener or George Clooney. Just get yours!*

Peter: *I wish I had the wisdom to tell a woman how to enjoy her orgasm more. I have never been with a woman who could reach orgasm quickly and easily. I think I'm pretty good about spending as much time as necessary to make it happen and I'm willing to do anything to make it happen, but it never seems as easy for them as it is for me. I'd give anything to have a "trick" or a technique that was guaranteed to make a woman come, because it is soooooo nice when she has that orgasm. It makes me feel good, too. If there is such a trick, let me in on the secret.*

Ray: *Let go! Just totally let go!*

The Goddess Orgasm Questionnaire for Women

The following questions were asked of dozens of women, whose answers helped me to write this book. Many of the respondents reported that just filling out the questionnaire was beneficial to them in understanding their own sexual response. Before they answered the questions, they hadn't given all that much thought to their own pleasure or put into writing what got them off, what didn't, how they felt about their orgasms, or what their orgasms mean to them. Because of those comments, I've decided to include the questionnaire itself for my readers to use as a tool to help them identify and explore intimate issues about their own orgasm experiences.

What is your favorite way to have an orgasm? (Pleasuring yourself, with your partner inside you, with a vibrator, from receiving oral sex, some other method.) Describe.

Do you use a vibrator? When? How often? Alone? With a partner? What do you like about it if you use one?

Do you have a favorite time of day or night that you enjoy to either pleasure yourself or have sex or make love?

Do you feel you have different kinds of orgasms? Describe them if they are different.

Do you have a position or a technique you prefer or rely on that almost always guarantees you an orgasm?

Is it pleasurable for you to have your clitoris directly stimulated? What about after you've had an orgasm? Do you prefer your clitoris not be touched at that point because it is too sensitive?

Do you masturbate/pleasure yourself? If so, when, where, and under what circumstances?

How has your self-pleasuring repertoire/routine/technique changed or evolved over time?

Are sex toys part of your self-pleasuring or with-a-partner experiences?

If you enjoy using sex toys, how often do you upgrade your equipment?

Describe the most intense orgasm you recall having. Describe the sensation itself and what the circumstances were. Were you alone, with someone, what was the physical location, were there any special conditions or circumstances? Was the position different or were you doing something you hadn't done before? Describe any atmosphere or conditions that might have contributed to this orgasm being special.

Do you believe you've ever had a G-spot or Grafenberg-spot orgasm? What did it feel like?

Have you ever had an orgasm as a result of a part of your body other than your genitals being directly stimulated? For example, having your toes sucked, your breasts/nipples stimulated, your earlobes nibbled . . .

Do you think you've had separate/different orgasmic experiences from a vaginal orgasm as compared to a clitoral orgasm?

Do you have an orgasm every day? More than once a day? Once a week, a month, a year? Never? Have you ever had an orgasm? And how do you know you did?

Do you regard orgasm to be a tension releaser?

What happens to you after orgasm? Are you more alert and awake or do you feel languorous and ready to fall asleep?

Have you ever found orgasm to be a relief from PMS pain?

If you are having an intimate sexual experience with a partner, how important is it to you that you have your orgasms together? What do you do to make this happen?

As a result of the "feel good" chemicals/endorphins released into the brain following orgasm, have you personally experienced a kind of euphoria or "lift" after orgasm? How long does the euphoria last?

Have you ever experienced a "big gush" at orgasm, what some sexual researchers have described as a "female ejaculation"?

What do you fantasize about when you pleasure yourself? What is your favorite "movie" or image that you play in your head? How often do you change the reel?

What do you enjoy most about orgasm?

Shopping Guide

The following are ideas and places to shop for many of the vibrators, G-spot finders, toys, and sex aids described in *The Goddess Orgasm*.

Personal lubricants (water-based liquids and gels that ease penetration) such as K-Y Liquid, Astroglide, and Vagisil Intimate Lubricant can be bought at any drugstore.

Vaginal moisturizers (products intended to alleviate vaginal dryness that are absorbed into the skin) such as Replens, Silken Secret, Moist Again, and K-Y Long Lasting are also available at drugstores. Most of them come packaged for single-use application, and some of them come with an applicator.

Vaginal creams meant to soothe and build estrogen levels in the vagina and thicken vaginal tissue like Premarin Cream and Estrace Cream contain estrogen and are available by doctor's prescription.

Vaginal rings such as Estring and Femring, which contain estrogen and stay in the vagina for up to three months, are also available only by doctor's prescription.

Vaginal tablets like Vagifem are inserted into the vagina once daily for two weeks and then twice a week thereafter. They contain estrogen and are used for building up levels of estrogen in the vagina. This product is popular with menopausal women, although it does not treat hot flashes. Vaginal tablets are available only by doctor's prescription.

Over-the-counter herbal and natural estrogen creams claim to replace lost estrogen and ease vaginal dryness. There are many products: too many to name. They are available at health food stores and on the Internet. Their efficacy has not been proven.

Many first-rate toys and vibrators can be found for purchase on the Web through California Exotic Novelties at www.calexotics.com. as well as the website adamandeve.com

Candida Royalle's superior and highly sensual line of female-oriented adult movies can be found on the Web at www.royalle.com. On her site, you will find much more than films. Ms. Royalle's movies and her Natural Contours personal massager can be ordered on the phone, as well, from her toll-free number, 1-800-456-LOVE [5683].

References

$\mathcal{T}$he *Goddess Orgasm* is not a rigorously researched book in the usual sense. I based my writing on ideas that developed from my own head and my own personal sexual experiences, which, um, have been myriad. I also relied on the stories and personal observations of many of my closest friends, whom I consider to be modern goddesses. My agent also put me in touch with other women who wanted to share their orgasm experiences with other women, in the hopes that one day all women would be able to achieve orgasmic bliss.

Other sources used in the writing of this book include the following:

Bodansky, Vera and Steve. *Extended Massive Orgasm*. Alameda, California: Hunter House, 2004.

D'Aulaire, Ingri, and Edgar Parin. *Book of Greek Myths*. Garden City, New York: Zephyr Books, Doubleday and Company, Inc., 1962.

Harris, Frank. *My Life and Loves*. New York: Grove Press, 1963.

King, Patricia, Ph.D., Sile Deady, and Gina Sigillito. *The Wisdom of the Celts*. New York: Citadel Press, 2004.

Ladas, Alice Kahn, Beverly Whipple, and John D. Perry, *The G-Spot*, New York: 1981.

Sex and the City, Home Box Office, Inc.

About the Author

*E*ve Marx, M.A., is the author of *What's Your Sexual IQ?* from Citadel. She is also the author of *View from the Porch: Tales from the Anti-Hamptons* and two sex how-to books, *Passion* and *10 Nights of Passion*. A graduate of Columbia University Teacher's College, Marx was an editor of *Penthouse Forum* and *Swank* magazines. For many years, under her pseudonym Mary Arno, she reviewed adult films for *AVN* and *Swank Video World*. Today she is a newspaper columnist and lifestyle and real estate writer for *The Record-Review*, *The Westchester County Times*, *The Fairfield County Times*, *The Pet Gazette*, and other regional publications. She lives in New York with her family.